ROUTLEDGE LIBRARY EDITIONS: LIBRARY AND INFORMATION SCIENCE

Volume 42

HUMAN RESOURCES MANAGEMENT IN LIBRARIES

HUMAN RESOURCES MANAGEMENT IN LIBRARIES

Edited by
GISELA M. WEBB

LONDON AND NEW YORK

First published in 1989 by The Haworth Press, Inc.

This edition first published in 2020
by Routledge
2 Park Square, Milton Park, Abingdon, Oxon OX14 4RN

and by Routledge
52 Vanderbilt Avenue, New York, NY 10017

Routledge is an imprint of the Taylor & Francis Group, an informa business

© 1989 The Haworth Press, Inc.

All rights reserved. No part of this book may be reprinted or reproduced or utilised in any form or by any electronic, mechanical, or other means, now known or hereafter invented, including photocopying and recording, or in any information storage or retrieval system, without permission in writing from the publishers.

Trademark notice: Product or corporate names may be trademarks or registered trademarks, and are used only for identification and explanation without intent to infringe.

British Library Cataloguing in Publication Data
A catalogue record for this book is available from the British Library

ISBN: 978-0-367-34616-4 (Set)
ISBN: 978-0-429-34352-0 (Set) (ebk)
ISBN: 978-0-367-37616-1 (Volume 42) (hbk)
ISBN: 978-0-367-37621-5 (Volume 42) (pbk)
ISBN: 978-0-429-35529-5 (Volume 42) (ebk)

Publisher's Note
The publisher has gone to great lengths to ensure the quality of this reprint but points out that some imperfections in the original copies may be apparent.

Disclaimer
The publisher has made every effort to trace copyright holders and would welcome correspondence from those they have been unable to trace.

Human Resources Management in Libraries

Gisela M. Webb
Editor

The Haworth Press
New York • London

Human Resources Management in Libraries has also been published as *Journal of Library Administration,* Volume 10, Number 4 1989.

© 1989 by The Haworth Press, Inc. All rights reserved. No part of this work may be reproduced or utilized in any form or by any means, electronic or mechanical, including photocopying, microfilm and recording, or by any information storage and retrieval system, without permission in writing from the publisher. Printed in the United States of America.

The Haworth Press, Inc., 10 Alice Street, Binghamton, NY 13904-1580
EUROSPAN/Haworth, 3 Henrietta Street, London WC2E 8LU England

Library of Congress Cataloging-in-Publication Data

Human resources management in libraries / Gisela M. Webb, editor.
   p. cm.
  Previously published as Journal of library administration, v. 10, no. 4, 1989.
  Includes bibliographies.
  ISBN 0-86656-938-3
  1. Library personnel management. I. Webb, Gisela M.
Z682.H84   1989
023—dc20   89-11211
                                                                                      CIP

Human Resources Management in Libraries

CONTENTS

Introduction *Gisela M. Webb*	1
The Role of Library Education in Meeting the Personnel Needs of Public and School Libraries *Teresa Heyser* *Richard G. Heyser*	3
Integrating Public and Technical Services Staffs to Implement the New Mission of Libraries *Jennifer Cargill*	21
Challenges for Information Services Librarians to Meet the Needs of an Information-Based Society *Frances Benham*	33
Allocation of Staff in the Academic Library: Relevant Issues and Consideration of a Rationale *Donald G. Frank*	47
Creating a New Classification System for Technical and Supervisory Library Support Staff *Lucy R. Cohen*	59
Training for Change: Staff Development in a New Age *Anne Grodzins Lipow*	87

The Technicolor Coat of the Academic Library Personnel
  Officer: The Evolution from Paper-Pusher
  to Policy Maker 99
    Dana C. Rooks

Accountability of Human Resource Professionals 115
    Frances O. Painter

Introduction

HUMAN RESOURCES MANAGEMENT IN LIBRARIES: ARE WE PREPARING TO PLAY AN ACTIVE ROLE IN THE EMERGING INFORMATION AGE?

"Organizations are only as good as the people who work for them" is an often quoted statement. As the private and nonprofit sectors are entering an era of competition, internationalization, shortages of highly qualified labor, and demands for excellence from customers, a renewed sense for the importance of human resources emerges. Books like *In Search of Excellence* have popularized the knowledge that companies which thrive in an era of increased competition hire "the Best and the Brightest," invest in the continuing education of their employees, create organizations which reward and reinforce creativity and entrepreneurship, are constantly scanning their environments for new developments and trends, and become partners with the institutions which educate their future employees.

As the Information Age unfolds, librarians have the unique opportunity to make their profession one of the most important forces in shaping this new era. Through the ages we have collected, organized, disseminated, and conserved the products of civilizations. In the process we have developed information ethics, philosophies, skills, and technologies which will enable us now to assume truly professional responsibilities, if we seize the opportunity.

In this issue library educators, managers, and staffs are sharing their opinions regarding the kinds of people we need to attract to the profession and what competencies are required in the new age. They will address, philosophically and practically, the human resources implications of the changing mission of libraries. The challenges faced by information services, the need to reallocate, reclassify, and retrain existing staff, and the increasingly important role human resources specialists play in libraries in transition are discussed. While our deficiencies and shortcomings are accurately analyzed and reiterated, the articles also convey a sense of optimism about the future, a trust in our abilities as professionals to live up to the challenges ahead, and respect for the people we work with. Librarians are preparing on all fronts to be active participants in the new age and success will follow.

Gisela M. Webb

The Role of Library Education in Meeting the Personnel Needs of Public and School Libraries

Teresa Heyser
Richard G. Heyser

The curriculum of schools of library and information science, as well as the suitability of their graduates for employment are topics that have been, and hopefully will continue to be, discussed. This paper further addresses these aforementioned issues by discussing the competencies needed by entry-level professionals in public libraries and school library media centers, and the present and future role of schools of library and information science in providing employers with fully qualified professionals.

PUBLIC LIBRARY COMPETENCIES

The size of public libraries range from the very small (those libraries serving a population under 10,000) to the very large (those serving a population over 1,000,000). This wide range of sizes brings about a wide range of programs, services and needs, particularly for qualified, competent personnel.

The "NCES Survey of Public Libraries, 1982: Final Report" provides invaluable data about public libraries in the United States. Among the data discussed are information concerning library personnel which helps present a picture of libraries in terms of number of personnel currently employed. For example, the 8,597 public

---

Dr. Teresa Heyser has taught at library schools at the University of Texas and Austin and Peabody College, Nashville, TN. Dr. Richard G. Heyser is Assistant Director of Library Services at Tarrant County Junior College, Fort Worth, TX.

© 1989 by The Haworth Press, Inc. All rights reserved.

libraries employed 92,179 individuals, of which 37,570 (40.8 percent) were professionals; 49,283 (53.5 percent) were technical, clerical, and other staff; and 5,325 (5.8 percent) were plant operation and maintenance staff.[1]

By surveying managers of public libraries, Herbert White and Marion Paris identified recommended courses, that is, courses which were deemed essential for professionals to have upon beginning, at an entry level, work with a public library. The recommended courses presented for small, medium and large public libraries are presented as Table 1. From the recommended courses identified by White and Paris, a curriculum track for public librarians was outlined. The curriculum track consists of: basic reference, advanced reference, children's services, collection development, materials for adults, materials for children, materials for young adults, public libraries, personnel management, introduction to information science, organization of materials—Dewey, general technical services and cataloging of nonbook materials.[2] It is important to note that the curriculum track for public libraries only had a 46 percent overlap with the curriculum track for academic libraries, and no curriculum track could be identified for special libraries.[3] A core curriculum consisting of basic reference, collection development, public libraries and introduction to information science was identified by the study for public libraries.[4]

Nathan Smith, Maurice Marchant and Laura Nielsen found somewhat different needs than those identified by White and Paris. Present needs (the study was reported in 1984) included general reference, bibliography, organizational, human relations, and research skills. They also pointed out that in 5 years library automation and online retrieval skills would join reference, human relations and research as skills needed by entry-level professionals. Responding public library directors noted that while most entry-level professionals possessed acceptable reference and bibliography skills, only a few had the desired computer, supervisory and business skills.[5]

Sara Laughlin identified the small public library staff's educational needs as falling into three areas: operations, management and leadership. Operations included tasks such as book selection/deselection, cataloging and processing or circulation. Management

TABLE 1

RECOMMENDED COURSES (Medians of 2.5 or below)
BY RESPONDENT GROUPS

Large Public Libraries (N=34) (60+ professional staff)	Medium Public Libraries (N=49) (20-59 professional staff)
Basic reference Advanced reference Children's services Adult services Storytelling Collection development Materials for adults Materials for children Materials for young adults Public libraries Introduction to information science Organization of materials - Dewey General technical services Cataloging of nonbook materials	Basic reference Advanced reference Children's services Young adult services Adult services Collection development Advanced collection development Materials for children Public libraries Library management Personnel and human relations Introduction to information science General online searching Organization of materials - Dewey Advanced cataloging and classification General technical services Cataloging of nonbook materials

Small Public Libraries (N=49) (4-19 professional staff)
Basic reference Advanced reference Children's services Young adult services Adult services Storytelling Collection development Materials for adults Materials for children Materials for young adults Public libraries Library management Personnel and human relations Library finance Organization of materials-Dewey General technical services

Source: Herbert S. White and Marion Paris, "Employer Preferences and the Library Education Curriculum," The Library Quarterly 55 (January 1985): 8-9.

tasks would include budgeting, staffing, problem solving, building maintenance, collection management and evaluation of staff and services. Leadership tasks would include staff, community and board relations, funding development, planning for change and lobbying. Laughlin further noted that while library education should cover all three areas, it should emphasize the development of leadership skills.[6]

Trends which indicate possible directions for future developments in the education of public library professionals are also becoming evident. The trends must be monitored to ensure that the students being graduated are equipped, not only to meet existing needs, but also to provide leadership for the future. Donald Sager cites trends identified by reviewing advertisements for public library positions and informal discussions with the administrators of large public libraries. Among them he notes the difficulty in recruiting and retaining children's librarians, automation specialists and competent middle management; a decline in extension and outreach programs; and reduced funding for innovative programming and the extension of existing services.[7]

Participants in the OCLC Conference on the Future of the Public Library also developed a list of anticipated trends. Among them are: library circulation and other services will be fully automated and self-service provided; library reference delivery will be replaced by fee-based information providers; market research will be used to make the best use of limited resources; librarians will focus on interpreting, selecting, judging and advising instead of merely providing access to the increasing amounts of information, and there will be an increasing division between the haves and have-nots.[8]

The time of taking for granted public support of public libraries has ended. Nothing demonstrates this fact more clearly than the recent closing of the Shasta County (California) Public Library System. Thomas J. Hennen, Jr. reports:

> Many librarians, it appears, are unwilling to even identify, much less take, the necessary calculated risks to make libraries truly necessary in 21st century America. Public libraries may have a future only because they already exist, not because there is any compelling need for them.[9]

Library education must be sure it provides professionals capable of exercising leadership if the public library is to do more than simply survive.

SCHOOL LIBRARY COMPETENCIES

According to the new standards for school library media centers, the purpose of the media program in the school is to ensure that students, faculty and staff are effective users of ideas and information.[10] To this end, the school library media program must be integrated into the schools' curriculum. By providing the resources to assist students in becoming proficient seekers and users of information, the school library media program plays an integral part in the educational process. Karen Whitney, President of the American Association of School Librarians, stresses that the school library media program "is a critical element in students' intellectual development, in promoting the love of learning, and in conveying the importance of using and evaluating information throughout life."[11]

To accomplish the mission or purpose set forth in the new school library media standards, the school media professional must provide:

1. Intellectual access to information through systematic learning activities which develop cognitive strategies for selecting, retrieving, analyzing, evaluating, synthesizing, and creating information at all age levels and in all curriculum content areas;

2. Physical access to information through (a) a carefully selected and systematically organized collection of diverse learning resources, representing a wide range of subjects, levels of difficulty, communication formats, and technological delivery systems; (b) access to information and materials outside the library media center and the school building through such mechanisms as interlibrary loan, networking, and other cooperative agreements, and online searching of databases; and (c) providing instruction in the operation of equipment necessary to use the information in any format;

3. Learning experiences that encourage users to become discriminating consumers and skilled creators of information through introduction to the full range of communications media and use of the new and emerging information technologies;

4. Leadership, instruction, and consulting assistance in the use of instructional and information technology and the use of sound instructional design principles;

5. Resources and activities that contribute to lifelong learning, while accommodating a wide range of differences in teaching and learning styles and in instructional methods, interests, and capacities;

6. A facility that functions as the information center of the school, as a locus for integrated, interdisciplinary, intergrade, and school-wide learning activities;

7. Resources and learning activities that represent a diversity of experiences, opinions, social and cultural perspectives, supporting the concept that intellectual freedom and access to information are prerequisite to effective and responsible citizenship in a democracy.[12]

Quality school media programs can be brought about by the positive leadership, sound planning, and effective and efficient management of human and physical resources of well-trained school media professionals.

Information Power: Guidelines for School Library Media Programs states that

> school library media specialists have a broad undergraduate education with a liberal arts background and hold a master's degree or equivalent from a program that combines academic and professional preparation in library and information science, education, management, media, communications theory, and technology. The academic program of study includes some directed field experience in a library media program, coordinated by a faculty member in cooperation with an experienced library media specialist.[13]

Are graduate schools of library and information science adequately preparing school library media professionals to provide the high quality of school library media programs outlined in *Information Power: Guidelines for School Library Media Programs*? According to the President of the American Association of School Librarians, Karen A. Whitney, school library media specialists just entering the field often are not adequately prepared to assume the wide range of responsibilities associated with directing exemplary school media programs.[14] Likewise, Karen K. Niemeyer, in *Education for Professional Librarians*, points out areas that are traditionally neglected by schools of library and information science in the preparation of school library media specialists. She suggests that existing courses should be carefully examined and the areas of emphasis modified. Since the best school library media specialists need a combination of "people skills" and professional knowledge, Niemeyer calls for library and information science programs to include units on self-confidence, teaching skills, leadership and management skills, image development, guidelines for dress, and stress management techniques.[15] Coursework should also include the development of positive attitudes toward continued professional development, according to William E. Hug.[16] The range of skills, knowledge, and attitudes required of a school library media professional must be continually updated and expanded. This can be accomplished through a variety of formal and informal professional development experiences throughout one's career.[17]

In conclusion, in order to bring about a positive change in the media programs of this nation's schools, the school library media professional must be viewed as a person with authority. "Those planning to enter the field must move from the traditional style of static aloofness to one of dynamic involvement in the educational process."[18] To meet the growing, changing information demands of our schools, library and information science programs must graduate "enthusiastic, informed school library media specialists who are people-oriented, curriculum-supportive, leadership-wise, and management-trained."[19]

LIBRARY EDUCATION

Quality of Students Attracted

According to Herbert S. White, there is definitely a problem with the student population in library and information science schools. The problem being that the students attracted to LIS programs are not the kinds of people many employers wish to hire. Employers today are emphasizing interpersonal communication skills, management aptitude, and entrepreneurial risk-taking. To a large degree, librarianship is still perceived as a haven for those who have an interest in ideas, who like to read, who are introverted and passive, and who have some aversion to people.[20] There is a shortage of applicants with backgrounds and aptitudes in the physical and hard social sciences, in computer science and in management.[21] Griffiths and King also found that there were not enough people with scientific backgrounds entering the library and information science profession.[22]

In an unpublished study (1988), Faibisoff and Salisu make several recommendations which library and information science programs might consider in attracting more students with the desirable backgrounds and aptitudes needed to meet the needs of the information society of the future. Those recommendations are:

1. If library schools wish to attract and recruit students with backgrounds other than those in the humanities and education, information about the library and information profession should be published in other disciplines.
2. Library and information science as a career should be more aggressively brought to the attention of undergraduate students.
3. Library schools in collaboration with professional associations and practitioners must develop publicity programs that promote the profession in such a way so that an increasing number of students will be attracted to it. Professional advertising agencies are really needed to promote this profession and provide it with an image that is as attractive as other professional careers.
4. Career opportunities in the profession should be promoted not only at the college level, but as early as the secondary school level of education.[23]

To increase enrollment of desirable students, Griffiths and King suggest that concerted efforts be made to present the profession as an exciting, forward-moving opportunity that epitomizes the challenges and the opportunities of the Information Age.[24]

COMPETENCIES OF THE FUTURE INFORMATION PROFESSIONAL

All information professionals trained for the future, regardless of work setting, must acquire certain types of knowledge, develop transferrable skills, and develop positive and other essential attitudes toward the profession, themselves, and others. Considering the diverse needs of different sectors of the information society, and evolving technology that will support delivery of future information services, a number of competencies have been identified through the literature which the information professional of the future must develop. These include knowledge, skills and attitudes necessary to the satisfactory performance of information work.

Buckland suggests that the ideal information professional should have the following combination of traits: (1) skills in technical matters related to information handling, such as indexing, programming, and cost analysis; (2) an orientation towards serving people; and (3) leadership and management abilities which include interpersonal skills, a sense of mission, and a concern for tactics and strategy.[25]

Some of the types of knowledge required of the information professional, as identified in the Griffiths and King study, are knowledge of the structure and organization of information; management of information; knowledge of information handling technologies, techniques, and methods; and knowledge of the information environment and trends occurring within this environment.[26] Other competencies required of the information professional are the ability to communicate well in a variety of modes; the ability to manage time effectively; a willingness to take or accept responsibility; and a responsiveness to time constraints. Griffiths and King suggested that these competencies be developed during the formal education process.[27]

In addition to the traditional skills associated with acquiring, organizing, and disseminating information, David Bender states that the information professional of tomorrow be able to assimilate and interpret information, evaluate data, extrapolate trends, and reach conclusions. He also believes future information professionals should possess superior personnel management and decision-making skills along with the ability to analyze and evaluate procedures and perform advanced system analysis, the ability to develop new applications for technology, and the ability to develop new products and services.[28] Kathleen Heim identifies developing a broad command of the organization of knowledge—its creation, diffusion, and use by different client groups; developing an intense commitment to providing access to information efficiently; and developing an attitude of openness to change as major competencies of the future information professional.[29] Other important attributes to be developed by information professionals are an attitude that is future-oriented, positive, opportunistic, and people-centered and knowledge of the economics of information and policy issues.[30] A search of the literature yields other attitudes found extremely important to work performances, including flexibility, patience, a sense of humor, persistence, sensitivity, and an inquiring mind.[31]

Griffiths and King identified the need for people with specific subject backgrounds, particularly in the scientific and technical disciplines, as one of the major requirements of the information professional.[32] Their project also indicates that the information professional of the future must be much more outgoing and proactive than in the past.[33] And, too, the information profession needs people who are capable of coping with a changing world, and of understanding how the competencies they acquire and develop can be utilized.[34]

IMPLICATIONS FOR PREPARATION OF LIBRARIANS

Society's means of accessing and acquiring information are changing rapidly with advances in technology and ever-expanding information needs. According to Gardner, library schools cannot ignore this nor the fact that libraries no longer dominate the information market, but must share it with an increasing number and variety of information suppliers. Schools of library and information science must adapt their curricula to these needs.[35] Gardner stresses the necessity of preparing students to design information systems, to manage and market information systems, to create and market data banks, to develop online searching ability, to analyze information, and to guarantee the quality of the information they provide.[36]

Jean Tague offers the following statement concerning new curriculum needs of library and information science programs: "Such topics as human information processing, interpersonal communications, the economics of information, local, national and global information systems, and the validity of information models must form part of the curriculum."[37] Bearman discusses several implications of the changing and information science. She, like Gardner, sees one such implication as the need to rethink the curricula of these programs, but she also sees the need to rethink the entrance requirements as well. A curriculum designed to educate information professionals of the future should include "courses on organization theory, financial planning, strategic planning, and effective communications."[38]

Another implication discussed by Bearman is the need for library schools to provide increased resources so that students can gain adequate hands-on experience in online searching, using microcomputers, participating in teleconferencing, and working with videodisks.[39] Bearman believes information professionals could be better qualified if there is more interaction among library and information science educators, practitioners, and professionals in related areas, such as business schools, computer science and communication departments.[40] Resnik, too, believes that library and information science educators can produce better qualified information professionals through interdisciplinary efforts which include the schools of business and social sciences.[41] Lewis concludes that schools of library and information science are probably not putting enough emphasis on the concept of the developing information market(s), the emerging information society, and sound information management. He states, "To fill existing needs schools should introduce short, sharp courses, specific seminars and conferences, special interest group events, distance learning developments, and informal groupings."[42] Unruh makes an excellent point when she stresses that schools of library and information science should make certain that the faculty teaching technology courses be truly knowledgeable about both practice and theory and be able to relate this to the students so that they can understand it.[43]

Kathleen Heim expresses a different view when she states "All that is required of our schools is development of an attitude of openness to change. We must simply ensure that the adaptation process to technological innovation is folded into the philosophies with which we imbue our students."[44]

ROLE OF LIBRARY EDUCATION IN CONTINUING PROFESSIONAL DEVELOPMENT

The fast-paced, ever-increasing, ever-changing information environment demands continuing professional development as a way of life for information professionals. As technology and the value of information change, professional development providers such as universities, employers, professional associations, corporations and information vendors, will play a prominent role in the continuing education of information professionals.[45] According to Kathleen Heim, it will be necessary for information professionals to return to the university for re-education. This need for periodic re-education should be a major emphasis of library and information science programs in the basic preparation of new information professionals.[46] Schools of library and information science seem the natural providers of continuing education for information professionals. LIS educators could design and implement offerings for formal, in-depth education through institutes, seminars, workshops, and short courses which would provide special-purpose training in particular skills or in particular technologies.[47]

In order to respond to these continuing education and professional development needs of their graduates, library and information science educators must be willing and able to provide professionals with education and training that fits not only the learners' needs, but also their demands for convenience.[48] However, it should be noted that while continuing education may be supported and applauded, White and Paris found there was little insistence on it and little reward for it, and thus the initiative to participate in it must come from the individual. White and Paris noted that the exception to this is the recent efforts of the Medical Library Association to tie continuing education to continuing certification.[49]

Professors in library and information science education can be a powerful influence toward building the desire for lifelong, professional improvement, and should strive to do so. They should further strive to ensure that the library school plays a leadership role in the provision of professional development programs.

THE FUTURE

An exact description of the future of library education in preparing entry-level professionals is impossible. However, forecasting based on the lessons of the past is a must if indeed we want to not only be prepared for the future, but also to lead the way into it. Michael Buckland identifies three categories into which librarianship can be sorted with respect to change. These categories are library values, library technology and library science. Library values refer to social values so they influence professional issues and library policy; for example, the role of the librarian and the mission of the library service. Library technology refers to technology available for use in library service and is concerned with the handling of physical things. Library science refers to the understanding of librarianship.[50] Buckland further states that the curriculum of the future can be expected to contain the following basic overlapping elements:

1. The role of information in society and of library services;
2. The needs, information-gathering behavior and institutional contexts of groups to be served, e.g., students, researchers, children, the aged, and so on;
3. The theory and practice of information retrieval-cataloging, classification, indexing, bibliography, etc.; and
4. The managerial, political and technological means most likely to be useful in developing and providing good library service.[51]

Herbert White writes that forecasting the future of library and information science education is difficult because of the impact practitioners, the larger academic community and the general public has on it.[52] White notes a list of alternatives, all with drawbacks. The alternatives include lengthening degree requirements beyond one year; adding prerequisite requirements; implementing a prerequisite undergraduate degree program; implementing a career option undergraduate degree program leading to non-MLS-requiring jobs;

specializing the one-year program preparing graduates to work in specific settings; or moving to a free market environment with no controls.[53] White, noting the drawbacks of the alternatives, proposes having stronger accreditation standards; maintaining the master's degree as the basic professional education preparation by lengthening the degree requirement beyond one year as rewards for doing so warrant and by viewing undergraduate courses and curricula with care and caution; and by keeping the graduate degree as a qualification for entry into the profession.[54]

Toni Carbo Bearman in summarizing the symposium for *Library Hi Tech* on "Educating the Future Information Professional" noted that most symposium participants emphasized the need for information professionals to be able to manage and use technology as a tool—"a means to an end, but not an end itself."[55] Bearman summarized that there was a need to better identify and agree upon competencies necessary for the future; that education required the harmony of all key components—from educator to practitioner; that additional resources must be obtained; and that strong continuing education programs must be developed.[56]

SUMMARY/CONCLUSION

There is no doubt but that the role of the librarian and other information professionals has changed and will continue to change, not only in public and school libraries, but also in all other branches of library and information science. Library education must not only react to change, but also must foresee and plan for it. Library education, if it is to succeed, must be active and responsive in several areas. Library education must work closely with library and information practitioners and their professional associations. Library education must take a leadership role in library and information science. The competencies needed by practitioners must be more clearly identified and constantly evaluated. Efforts must be made to attract a wider variety of students into library and information science programs, particularly from science and technology. And, new methods of teaching/delivering information must be explored.

Librarianship in general, if it is to survive, must take on a much more active role. The all too true image of the passive/reactive librarian must come to an end, and strong leadership demonstrated if the profession is to survive.

NOTES

1. "The NCES Survey of Public Libraries, 1982: Final Report" in *The Bowker Annual of Library and Book Trade Information*, 31st edition, 1986 (New York: R. R. Bowker, 1986), 348.
2. Herbert S. White and Marion Paris, "Employer Preferences and the Library Education Curriculum," *The Library Quarterly* 55 (January 1985): 11.
3. Ibid., 10-11.
4. Ibid., 13.
5. Nathan, Smith, Maurice Marchant and Laura Nielsen, "Education for Public and Academic Librarianship: A View from the Top," *Journal of Education for Librarianship* 24 (Spring 1984): 233-245.
6. Sara Laughlin, "Small Public Libraries," in *Education for Professional Librarians* (White Plains, NY: Knowledge Industry Publications, 1986), 77.
7. Donald J. Sager, "Large Public Libraries," in *Education for Professional Librarians* (White Plains, NY: Knowledge Industry Publications, 1986), 28.
8. Thomas J. Hennen, Jr., "Public Librarians Take Cool View of Future," *American Libraries* 19 (May 1988): 392.
9. Ibid.
10. *Information Power: Guidelines for School Library Media Programs* (Chicago: American Library Association and Association for Education Communications and Technology, 1988), 1.
11. Karen A. Whitney, "President's Column," *School Library Media Quarterly* 16 no. 2 (Winter 1988): 82.
12. *Information Power*, 1-2.
13. Ibid., 59.
14. Whitney, 81.
15. Karen K. Niemeyer, "School Libraries and Media Centers," in *Education for Professional Libraries*, ed. Herbert S. White (White Plains, NY: Knowledge Industry Publications, 1986, 127-128.
16. William E. Hug, "School Library Media Education and Professional Development," *School Library Media Quarterly* 16 no. 2 (Winter 1988): 116.
17. Shirley L. Aaron, "The Role of Professional Development Activities in Promoting Improved Instructional Services in the Library Media Program," *School Library Media Quarterly* 16 no. 2 (Winter 1988): 84.
18. Niemeyer, 125.
19. Ibid., 138.
20. Herbert S. White, "Graduate Education for the Library Professional," in *Education for Professional Librarians*, ed. Herbert S. White (White Plains, NY: Knowledge Industry Publications, 1986), 189.
21. Ibid.

22. Jose-Marie Griffiths and Donald W. King, *New Directions in Library and Information Science Education* (White Plains, NY: Knowledge Industry Publications for American Society for Information Science, 1986), 259.

23. Sylvia G. Faibisoff and Taofiq M. Salisu, "Profile of Students at the University of Oklahoma," (1988), 22-23.

24. Griffiths and King, 260.

25. M. K. Buckland, "Education for Information Management," in *Education for Information Management: Directions for the Future, Record of a Conference*, May 1982, International Academy at Santa Barbara, 13-19.

26. Griffiths and King, 248.

27. Ibid., 252.

28. David Bender, "Educating the Future Information Professional," *Library Hi Tech* 5 (Summer 1987): 33.

29. Kathleen Heim, "Educating the Future Information Professional," *Library Hi Tech* 5 (Summer 1987): 33.

30. Dennis Lewis, "Educating the Future Information Professional," *Library Hi Tech* 5 (Summer 1987): 38.

31. Betty Unruh, "Educating the Future Information Professional," *Library Hi Tech* 5 (Summer 1987): 38.

32. Griffiths and King, 248.

33. Ibid., 259.

34. Ibid., 253.

35. Richard K. Gardner, "Library and Information Science Education: The Present State and Future Prospects," in *Education for Library and Information Professionals: Present and Future Prospects*, ed. Richard K. Gardner (Littleton, CO: Libraries Unlimited, 1987), 35.

36. Ibid., 36.

37. Ibid.

38. Toni Carbo Bearman, "The Changing Role of the Information Professional," *Library Trends* 32 (Winter 1984): 258-259.

39. Ibid.

40. Ibid.

41. Linda Resnik, "Educating the Future Information Professional," *Library Hi Tech* 5 (Summer 1987): 39.

42. Lewis, 39.

43. Unruh, 38.

44. Heim, 35.

45. Bender, 30.

46. Heim, 33.

47. Resnik, 37.

48. Ibid.

49. White and Paris, 20.

50. Michael K. Buckland, "Educating for Librarianship in the Next Century." *Library Trends* 34 (Spring 1986): 781.

51. Ibid., 785-786.

52. Herbert S. White, "The Future of Library and Information Science Education," *Journal of Education for Library and Information Science Education* 26 (Winter 1986): 175-177.

53. Ibid., 177-178.

54. Ibid., 179-180.

55. Toni Carbo Bearman, "Educating the Future Information Professional," *Library Hi Tech* 5 (Summer 1987): 28.

56. Ibid., 28-29.

Integrating Public and Technical Services Staffs to Implement the New Mission of Libraries

Jennifer Cargill

MISSION OF LIBRARIES NOW AND IN THE FUTURE

As technology has been introduced into libraries and access to information has become more available to the public, the mission of libraries has and will continue to change. While libraries will continue to acquire, process, service, and warehouse information in a variety of formats, databases will also increasingly be mounted on library and institutional networks, accessible to patrons with or without assistance from library staff. Librarians will find themselves doing more instruction in search strategies, performing fewer mediated searches, and providing online reference service. Libraries and librarians will remain the guardians of information; methods of accessing the information will continue to diversify.

At the same time, individuals' approach to work and leisure have been undergoing revision; job expectations have changed as a result. People accept that they will not remain in one position and with one organization their entire work careers. There is an understanding or realization that there is a high likelihood career choices will change during one's work life; it is very probable that people will experience two or more careers before retiring. Drastic interest digressions are possibilities; indeed they are realities as the environment of our lives change.

Jennifer Cargill is Associate University Librarian at Rice University, Houston, TX.

As librarians move toward becoming brokers of information in an information-reliant world, libraries approach to providing service, accessing databases, and disseminating information will be revised. The mechanism through which we make information available will become more critical. The constituencies served by academic libraries will broaden, become more demanding as their expectations rise, and will be more sophisticated. Academic libraries will find themselves competing with computing groups and other information brokers.

PHILOSOPHY OF LIBRARIANSHIP IN THE LAST QUARTER OF THIS CENTURY

As the mission of the library changes and librarians' expectations adjust as a result, the philosophy of librarianship will also evolve in those libraries which are progressive, those that are directed and staffed by people with vision and the courage to take risks. As more routine tasks are eliminated through shared databases, through the benefits of technology, and through delegation to support staff, librarians are freed for managerial responsibilities, coordination of staff, and assignments requiring special training or subject emphasis. Additional education will become required rather than simply being viewed as desirable.

For those of us currently in the field as practitioners, the next few decades will bring many changes. Some of us have already observed librarianship's evolution from a book-oriented profession in which librarians were trained as bookmen and the emphasis was on building the collection to a profession exploring its social consciousness and conscience. The profession has further evolved to one that was concentrating upon discovering and implementing technology to the present situation where economic realities are requiring us to move from warehousing to accessing information.

At the same time, our approach to human resources has changed to a recognition that to challenge people and to inspire them to provide better services, the work they perform should provide rewards. For many people this also means performing a variety of tasks, accompanied by responsibility and authority, rather than completing the same tasks repeatedly, primarily to earn a salary. In some libraries staff have been performing both public and technical services tasks for years. In other libraries, these activities have been kept strictly separate, with no overlap. Too often in those libraries, public service librarians were only marginally familiar with technical tasks and were even suspicious of the routines deemed necessary to acquire and process materials. Technical service librarians in turn were skeptical of the patron interaction workload experienced by the public service librarians.

RATIONALE FOR INTEGRATION

With technology blurring the lines between each area, it seems reasonable for the responsibilities to become similarly blurred, with overlapping activities. With more responsibilities moving from professional to support positions, more challenges to stimulate professionals will be needed. Some routines will be eliminated while still others are created, increasing the boredom factor and necessitating more diversity within positions in order to retain the interest of employees.

One alternative as tasks overlap more is the creation of multifunctional positions, integrating public and technical responsibilities within both professional and support positions. In addition, as the scarcity of librarians in some functional areas continues, designing multitasking into existing and new positions will help libraries bridge the skills gap. In some regions the economy may dictate that positions be redesigned with responsibilities consolidated in order to maintain effective service.

Today, in the latter part of the twentieth century, we are seeing increasing prices for library materials affecting our buying power. Even in areas where the economy is stable and unemployment is low, libraries, especially university libraries, are experiencing difficulties in adequately funding acquisition of all types of library materials. Parallel to this phenomenon is the initial cost of automating which for many libraries is coming at a time that funds are not readily available. It is, therefore, essential for libraries to utilize staff, especially the more costly administrative and professional staff, in as cost-effective a manner as possible. Delegating some routine tasks, that need not be handled by librarians, to support staff is one way to make effective use of library staff.

PLANNING FOR INTEGRATION

Once the integration of public and technical functions has begun to be explored, the concept must be "sold" to the rest of the library. Three primary library groups must be convinced: the library administration; middle managers; and the staff as a whole. In addition, colleagues in other similar libraries may initially question the concept.

Administration within the library. Within the library administration itself there may be a level of skepticism that arises from protectiveness of traditional divisional lines. Barriers to combining functions within position descriptions may be erected. The senior administrative group must be solidly behind the concept of integration of functions. Certainly the library director must believe in the concept. He/she may begin planning for the implementation with the departure or transfer of some of the associate/assistant directors. A person already in the senior ranks may have the background and skills to oversee the integration of functions.

Middle managers within the library. Similarly, the middle managers, who will be on the front lines implementing the new concept, may have reservations. The evolving philosophy of academic librarianship may be alien to everything the middle managers were taught in graduate school or have experienced thus far in their careers. They may lack confidence or skills to assume responsibilities in other areas or they may have staff who lack confidence and skills. The specter of undergoing additional training at this stage in a librarian's career may be daunting and some may even feel it is insulting. They may fear the consequences to their own work lives as the formerly stable, predictable library environment undergoes drastic changes.

Once the senior administrators are comfortable with the concept, the middle managers should be incorporated into the discussion and process of planning, with their support sought. Frustration with failing to recruit librarians for certain types of positions may encourage exploring integration of functions. Designing position descriptions for multitask vacancies and the successful recruitment of flexible individuals may be the impetus leading to their support.

Library staff. Finally, the library staff must be "sold" on the benefits that will accrue from establishing a new organizational pattern to better provide services to the library's constituency. New staff without preconceived ideas of the "correct" library structure will probably be more open to the multifunctional concepts. However, some new staff, fresh from library school courses in which they learned the "traditional" organizational patterns may be surprised by the expectations of the library which differ from those taught by their library science professors.

Colleagues in other libraries. On the periphery, carefully observing the integration process will be colleagues within the Profession. Those colleagues who are proponents of more traditional library structure will be skeptical of the changes being implemented. They may have also experienced or observed attempts at nontraditional structure that failed. They may also fear that if libraries are successful in integrating public and technical functions, the divisional structure within their own library will disappear and they will lose their "territory."

IMPLEMENTATION

How to approach the integration of public and technical service staffs? First, a careful assessment of the library and staff should be undertaken. This assessment should include organizational and institutional climate, managerial support, strengths and weaknesses of the staff, the level of interest in innovation, and support for change. An approach which will help with this analysis is detailed in one of the articles listed in background sources (Cargill, "Use of a Proactive Analysis Process in Human Resources Management").

Role of Administrators

Already mentioned is the necessity that the library's senior administrators agree that the concept is one they are interested in implementing. There should be thorough discussion of integration at this level, supported by background research, and a discussion of the analysis of the staff willingness and ability to implement the proposed structure. Next, the concept should be shared and discussed with middle management. Middle management should be involved in planning for the implementation. In fact, most of the actual planning should emanate from this level, under the direction of senior administrators. Some facilitating on the part of management consultants may be appropriate at this stage. The adoption of team management as a philosophy may soon prove supportive to integrating of public and technical functions. During the implementation process, the use of personal and expert power by administrators, rather than positional power, will facilitate the change process, though it should also be clear that the use of positional power may be necessary on occasion.

Role of Existing Staff

After consensus is reached among those who will be planning and directing the implementation, the sharing of the concept and requesting of support of staff in the implementation process should be discussed. All staff should be offered the opportunity for input. Similar models and their success and failure should be shared. A forum for questions to be directed toward management may be appropriate. Small discussion groups can be formed to discuss the present situation, the benefits of integration of functions, the obstacles that may arise, issues that should be addressed, and the likelihood of success. Every effort should be made to come as close as possible to consensus among staff.

Some staff, while openly stating their support of the concept of integrating public and technical services, may also feel threatened as they perceive their authority dwindling. Those who have felt they served the organization through a parental attitude toward other staff may find that this role is no longer appropriate. They may be tempted to test the new organization culture by manipulating emotionally dependent staff. If those same people have also helped mold the existing staff and have been instrumental in their being hired and promoted to better jobs, they may feel uneasy as they perceive they have less input into the now shared hiring and planning processes. There may be a lack of willingness to relinquish perceived or real authority and responsibility. In addition, as new staff with different skills and expectations are hired, these self-appointed organizational "parents" may feel they are losing "control." As the reliance on friendship networks dissipates, the network leaders may begin to feel their worth to the organization is diminishing.

Both the formal and informal leaders may be hesitant to relinquish the control they have had within the organization and over staff. Staff who have been the ones "always counted upon" will have to understand that leadership skills must be developed in others so reliance on just a few staff will no longer be necessary. If they continue to try to exercise the parental role, or attempt to keep staff dependent upon them, eventually they will find themselves regarded as barriers to change, and as individual who aren't team players but who are meddlers.

In short, existing staff must demonstrate a willingness to relinquish control, abandon their parental role, and cease being dependent upon a reliance on friends to make the organization work. Emotional and work dependence upon close friends will be detrimental to the success of the integration concept. Some attrition should be expected — and should be welcomed.

New Staff

The recruiting and hiring of new staff will be critical to the implementation of the integration of public and technical services. Positions must be redesigned, with reporting lines and authority levels clearly delineated. The vacancy announcements should clearly detail that the positions incorporate integration of public and technical functions. Flexible librarians, newly entering the profession, will be attracted to positions where they will have the opportunity to develop skills in more than one specialization. They will realize the benefits of having time to learn a variety of skills, delaying any decision about specialization to a later date. They will also see that these integrated positions provide an opportunity to prepare themselves for the evolutionary process that academic libraries are undergoing.

Some examples of integrated positions might include these:

- Cataloging and Documents, especially if the library inputs its documents into its online system and bibliographic utility.
- General Reference and Documents Reference. The payoff is having staff familiar with the entire reference collection.
- Acquisitions and General Reference. Again, collection needs and familiarity will benefit the Library.
- Cataloging and General Reference. Such a combination eliminates the common statement that people in one area don't understand the needs of the other area.

What to look for in newly hired staff? A healthy mental attitude, a willingness to be flexible, a desire to develop a variety of skills, and a diverse background are all critical traits needed for integration to be successful. Staff new to the organization should be quickly incorporated into the planning and implementing process. If committees or task forces are formed, these new staff should be included and encouraged to present their ideas.

BENEFITS

Benefits of the integration of public and technical functions will accrue to staff as well as to the organization. Careers of staff, especially the professionals, will be enhanced by the diversity of the skills acquired. Librarians will find they have more career options as a result of the training they receive in a library that has integrated functions. Their willingness to explore different ideas and take risks will be beneficial as they develop their own leadership skills.

The library itself will have more flexibility in work assignments with more staff to rely upon for staffing service desks and addressing processing backlogs. Priorities can be established and achieved with more staff in a position to assist in reaching goals. Some staff will have the skills to lead the change process forward while others will play an equally important role in the background, providing valuable support.

Economically the library will also benefit since the most highly paid staff will be concentrating on professional and managerial tasks, best utilizing the training they have received. Most of the routine tasks should be turned over to support staff and student assistants. The library will also have the economic benefit of the most appropriate staff being assigned to relevant tasks.

The profession will eventually benefit from an increasing number of librarians and support staff who are flexible, visionary, and are prepared to change as libraries and librarians evolve into new roles within society. Without vision and the courage to change, libraries and librarians will find themselves on the sidelines. Integrating traditional public and technical functions with library staffs will assist libraries in remaining effective information brokers.

Finally, the constituency the library serves will benefit from receiving service from flexible, highly skilled staff, knowledgeable about the full range of library services, and the collections. This will be particularly beneficial as patrons access information in ever-changing ways and one-to-one, appointment-based service becomes more prevalent. Dealing with well-trained, knowledgeable staff will reduce the frustrations of access data in a world experiencing an information explosion.

SUGGESTED BACKGROUND SOURCES

Arthur, Michael B., et al. *Working with Careers*. New York: Center for Research in Career Development, Graduate School of Business, Columbia University, 1984.

Atkinson, Hugh C. "The Impact of New Technology on Library Organization." *The Bowker Annual of Library & Book Trade Information*. 29th ed. New York: Bowker, 1984, pp. 109-114.

Battin, Patricia. "The Electronic Library: A Vision for the Future." *EDUCOM Bulletin*. 19 (Summer 1984): 12-17.

Beninger, James R. *The Control Revolution: Technological and Economic Origins of the Information Society*. Cambridge, MA: Harvard University Press, 1986.

Berg, Per-Olof. "Symbolic Management of Human Resources," *Human Resource Management*. 25 (Winter 1986): 557-79.

Busch, Joe. "Coming Out of the Back Room: Management Issues for Technical Services in the Eighties." *Technical Services Quarterly*. 2 (Spring-Summer 1985): 115-41.

Cargill, Jennifer. "Use of a Proactive Analysis Process in Human Resources Management." *Technical Services Quarterly*. 5 (Summer 1988):

_____ and Webb, Gisela. *Managing Libraries in Transition*. Phoenix, AZ: Oryx Press, 1988.

Cherrington, David S. *Work Ethics: Working Values and Values that Work.* New York: AMACOM, 1980.

Conroy, Barbara. "The Human Element: Staff Development in the Electronic Library." *Drexel Library Quarterly.* 18 (Fall 1981): 91-106.

Davis, Peter. "Libraries at the Turning Point: Issues in Proactive Planning." *Journal of Library Administration.* 1 (Summer 1980): 11-24.

Drucker, Peter F. "The Coming of the New Organization." *Harvard Business Review.* 66 (January-February 1988): 45-53.

Dwyer, James R. "The Evolutionary Role of Technical Services." *Journal of Library Administration.* 9 (1988): 13-26.

Euster, Joanne R. *The Academic Library Director: Management Activities and Effectiveness.* New York: Greenwood Press, 1987.

Fayen, Emily Gallup. "Beyond Technology: Rethinking 'Librarian'." *American Libraries.* 17 (April 1986): 240-2.

Fisher, K. Kim. "Management Roles in the Implementation of Participative Management Systems." *Human Resource Management.* 25 (Fall 1986): 459-79.

Freedman, Maurice J. "Automation and the Future of Technical Services." *Library Journal.* 109 (June 15, 1984): 1197-1203.

Gibson, Jane Whitney, and Hodgetts, Richard M. *Organizational Communications: A Managerial Perspective.* Orlando, FL: Academic Press, 1986.

Goldsmith, Vern. *Effective Team Building.* New York: American Management Associations Extension Institute, 1980.

Gorman, Michael. "The Ecumenical Librarian." *Reference Librarian.* 9 (Fall/Winter 1983): 55-64.

_____. "On Doing Away with Technical Services Departments." *American Libraries.* 10 (July/August 1979): 435-437.

Hendrick, Clyde. "The Library in the Twenty-First Century." *College and Research Libraries.* 47 (March 1986): 127-131.

Hyatt, James A., and Santiago, Aurora A. *University Libraries in Transition.* Washington, DC: National Association of College and University Business Officers, 1987.

Kanter, Rosabeth Moss. *The Change Masters: Innovation and Entrepreneurship in the American Corporation.* New York: Simon and Schuster, 1983.

Kets de Vries, Manfred et al. "Using the Life Cycle to Anticipate Satisfaction at Work." *Journal of Forecasting.* 3 (1984): 161-72.

Lewis, David W. "An Organizational Paradigm for Effective Academic Libraries." *College and Research Libraries.* 47 (July 1986): 337-53.

McCombs, Gillian. "Public and Technical Services: Disappearing Barriers." *Wilson Library Bulletin.* 61 (November 1986): 25-28.

Morf, Martin. *Optimizing Work Performance: A Look Beyond the Bottom Line.* New York: Quorum Books, 1986.

Olsgaard, John N. "Automation as a Socio-Organizational Agent of Change: An Evaluative Literature Review." *Information Technology and Libraries.* 4 (March 1985): 19-28.

Pascarella, Perry. *The New Achievers: Creating a Modern Work Ethic*. New York: Free Press, 1984.
Portnoy, Robert A. *Leadership: What Every Leader Should Know about People*. Englewood Cliffs, NJ; Prentice-Hall, 1986.
Rasberry, Robert W., and Lemoine, Laura Fletcher. *Effective Managerial Communication*. Boston: Kent Publishing, 1986.
Riggs, Donald E. *Library Leadership: Visualizing the Future*. Phoenix, AZ: Oryx Press, 1982.
──────. *Strategic Planning for Library Managers*. Phoenix, AZ: Oryx Press, 1984.
Shapero, Albert. *Managing Professional People*. New York: Free Press, 1985.
Webb, Gisela. "Educating Librarians and Support Staff for Technical Services." *Journal of Library Administration*. 9 (1988): 111-120.
Williams, James W. "The Decentralization of Selected Technical Services at the University of Illinois at Urbana-Champaign." *Technical Services Quarterly*. 4 (Summer 1987): 5-19.
Wynn, Richard and Guditus, Charles W. *Team Management: Leadership by Consensus*. Columbus, OH: Charles E. Merrill, 1984.
Yankelovich, Daniel. *New Rules, Searching for Self-Fulfillment in a World Turned Upside Down*. New York: Random House, 1981.
Yukl, Gary A. *Leadership in Organizations*. Englewood Cliffs, NJ: Prentice-Hall, 1981.

Challenges for Information Services Librarians to Meet the Needs of an Information-Based Society

Frances Benham

Transition and change are words used frequently to characterize the present era. A recent report prepared for the U.S. Congress by the Office of Technology Assessment projects that during the coming two decades new technologies, increases in foreign trade, and the values of a new generation can be expected to reshape every product, service, and job in the United States.[1] According to the report such forces will shake the very foundation of the most stable American business. The expected significant role of information during this period is explored in detail, but without mention of the involvement of libraries.

The words transition and change, nonetheless, also aptly describe the nation's academic and research libraries. Much of the change observable in libraries reflect that of forces external to the library, and as such, mirrors the general impact of automation on society. In little more than two decades libraries have utilized emerging technologies to improve dramatically the bibliographic control of library materials. This phenomenon, increasingly international in scope, makes technically feasible the long-held, though practically impossible, dream of complete bibliographic control. The significance of the degree to which librarians, publishers, archivists, academics, and funding agencies have electronically encoded the existing bibliographic record cannot be overstated. That achievement, continuing unabated, and far from complete, makes possible im-

---

Frances Benham is Associate Dean of Libraries for Collections and Information Services at the University of Alabama, Tuscaloosa, AL.

© 1989 by The Haworth Press, Inc. All rights reserved.

proved research efficiency and effectiveness coupled with new opportunities and responsibilities for librarians. Today librarians and scholars can identify with more certainty than ever what has been published; which, if any libraries own it; and whether and the degree to which it is accessible. This is true of both monographs and serials as well as of information in a variety of formats. It is especially true of currently produced material, and it is increasingly true of older publications.

EARLY EFFECTS OF AUTOMATION

A comparison of the activities of technical services departments of the 1960s and today reveals major changes in productivity and in the methods to achieve it. Fewer professionally educated personnel are engaged in cataloging, the huge backfiles of materials awaiting cataloging are a thing of the past in many libraries, paraprofessionals and clerks are engaged in more demanding and interesting work, and a number of the most tedious, boring, and error-prone manual tasks, such as filing, are being relegated to the computer. In retrospect the results indicate a striking transformation, though the process, occasionally endured in anguish, was relatively serene. By and large the transition was made with positive and energetic involvement as the potential of new systems was quickly recognized.

As the automated bibliographic infrastructure developed over the last two decades automation could be applied productively in library information services units. Circulation was an early beneficiary of that evolution. Those libraries switching from a manual to an automated circulation system experienced major, dramatic, and positive improvements. The benefits for libraries outweighed those difficulties encountered, however distressing they may have seemed at the time.

Access to the early cumbersome and expensive online databases, typically in the sciences, initially was provided in research libraries by a few trained librarians. With cost a significant determinant, relatively little use was made of such services. The OCLC interlibrary loan network, activated in 1979, dramatically affected the efficiency and volume of interlibrary sharing of materials simply by allowing libraries to identify accurately and communicate directly with specific owners of needed titles.

It is only within the last several years that the impact of library automation and electronic publishing have developed to a level that makes possible for information services the potential for change widely experienced in technical services by the early 1970s. Library information services today are poised to join the information revolution in earnest.

THE PACE OF CHANGE

Information services librarians can take encouragement in the realization that though modified roles will be necessary for the achievement of the full potential of the information age, the seeds of practical change rest in familiar functions and activities. Experience suggests that change generally is incremental—evolutionary rather than revolutionary, regardless of the potential of the tools at hand. The university, the institutional home of most of the research libraries of the nation, has remained remarkably stable in spite of the availability of technologies to drastically change and, many believe, to substantially improve the quality of the education it offers. Though it has incorporated many scientific and technical developments, the form, function, and societal position of today's university remains much the same as that of a century or more ago. Changes that have occurred have been gradual, often necessitated by social, economic, and political pressures—the same pressures which in other circumstances limit desirable change. Libraries, like their parent institutions, have and will continue to incorporate change, even at an accelerated pace, but at levels which will prove manageable for most of those involved. Far from fearful of change, today's library personnel chafe at constraints which limit the ability of their libraries to take advantage of technologies viewed as valuable in improving productivity and services.

As opportunities develop for change, librarians are challenged to examine each in the context of the mission of the local library and parent organization, the publishing universe germane to local needs, and the collections and services of other libraries and agencies which might prove beneficial to the library's clientele. With automation, network options increase sharing opportunities which have become vital to library services. Such cooperative ventures should never be viewed as alternatives for saving money but rather as opportunities to utilize resources wisely in the quest to serve clients more effectively. Yesterday's librarians were concerned with the local library and its collections; today's options include databases and collections to be shared at the state, regional, national, and international levels.

ROLE OF INFORMATION SERVICES LIBRARIANS

The development and continuing growth of the international bibliographic infrastructure impacts positively and dramatically on library information service activities including reference, collection development, user instruction, and database searching. Moreover, because these areas are highly interrelated it may be expected that libraries will increasingly seek out for employment those who can combine these skills in service to a particular discipline or subject. Julie Neway describes an evolving role in which librarians understand the knowledge habits of clients and are well versed in their subject areas. Assistance is provided such clients as needed through the task of analyzing, advising, liking, and training. Neway sees the library as but one of many places where information services librarians can participate as valued team members in research activities.[2] These librarians must be generalist enough to provide basic assistance for a range of client's needs as well as to possess the knowledge to refer those with specialized or in-depth subject needs. Subject specialist information services librarians will follow the literature of a field closely enough to know its major theories, trends, communication modes, compelling questions, and dominant figures, and they will be familiar with the holdings of many libraries in the assigned subject field.

Research libraries traditionally have provided these services in departmental and branch libraries, particularly in law, medicine, music, and the sciences. As well, there long have been librarians who by education and avocation have maintained high levels of specific subject knowledge alongside the requirements of more general job descriptions. Some academic libraries are moving in this direction and others have long employed subject specialists whose duties include the provision of client services.

COOPERATIVE COLLECTION DEVELOPMENT

It is increasingly important that information services librarians use the new bibliographic infrastructure and related tools to develop a clear picture of the universe of literature useful to a particular discipline. As no library can afford to develop a comprehensive collection in many, if any, subject, it is incumbent upon these librarians to maintain current awareness of the strengths and weaknesses of the local collection, and also of valuable collections of interest to their clients wherever such collections may be owned. This knowledge can serve as the basis for cooperative collection development so that all materials of potential importance in a field are owned, shared and needed, and preserved.

The RLG Conspectus was developed as a tool to aid collection development librarians in that task. Started in 1974, and rapidly gaining momentum since 1983, the Conspectus, as described by Paul Mosher and Nancy Gwinn, provides an overview of existing collection strengths and current and future collecting intentions in specific libraries.[3] Now online, the Conspectus is available to information services librarians who can search it by subject, class, language, institution, and collection level.[4] Not only can it serve to inform selection decisions, it can provide a guide to researchers, particularly to important older collections not yet fully cataloged on the major online databases. In the same fashion it can be utilized for interlibrary borrowing. It can guide a disciplined examination of the local collection, revealing pockets of strengths as well as gaps. It can serve as a reference tool to guide students and faculty to local strengths useful for research projects. It can prove useful in developing lists of collection areas to be targeted for priority attention in the event of disaster.[5] As new programs are proposed it can provide data useful in weighing the university's ability to adequately fund them. The Conspectus can aid in the improvement of cooperative collection management at the national level as involved libraries share collecting levels and accept primary collecting and preservation responsibilities for specific subject materials. Using current computer and telecommunication capabilities, libraries en masse have the potential cooperatively to identify, collect, service, maintain, and preserve most of the publications output of the world—a virtual impossibility without cooperation.

The growing wealth of articles and preservations about the Conspectus, its use, value, weaknesses, and possible alternatives to it, are healthy signs of the awareness of librarians of the significance of the topic of shared collection development. Its reported use by a variety of networks, and its use and consideration for use in other countries are positive signs of the impact of the idea and of its practical implementation and effect.

Resource sharing must be viewed by information services librarians as integral to their activities if effective service is to be provided. Those responsible for collection development must develop expertise in the use and communication methods of scholarship in the fields they serve.[6] Recognition of the importance of collection development activities in the work of information services is evidenced by the inauguration of a new section in the American Library Association's Reference and Adult Services Division. The rapid growth of membership in the new section suggests a high level of interest on the part of information services librarians in collections work. CODES (Collection Development and Evaluation Section) committees and discussion groups met with good attendance for the first time at last summer's ALA New Orleans Conference.[7]

THE JOURNAL DILEMMA

The problems of collecting and/or providing access to the monographic output of the world's authors is paralleled, if not surpassed, in magnitude by those surrounding the development of journal collections satisfactory to research needs. Academics publish in journals to record and disseminate knowledge, to gain prestige among their peers, and more pragmatically, to earn tenure and promotion in their home institutions. They gain little, if any, financial reward for their efforts, and often they or their departments must fund page charges when their articles are selected for publication. It is to their advantage to have their discoveries, ideas, wisdom, and knowledge disseminated as widely as possible. The scholarly journal, as it has existed since the eighteenth century, has served their needs reasonably well until recently, and relationships with publishers often have been satisfying and rewarding.

Publishers also have enjoyed this symbiotic relationship. They have utilized the editorial and authoring skills of academics to develop journals which are sold for profit, often to institutional libraries of the universities which employ the journals' authors. Over the last decade publishers in the commercial sector have increased subscription rates to such levels that library purchases of other materials and services have been affected adversely. Within the last several years the deletion of large numbers of titles from subscription lists coupled with concerted protests by faculty and the library profession appears to have curbed but not eliminated the escalation of journal prices.

Journal titles, deleted by budgetary response to spiraling price increases, are now held by fewer libraries. Interlibrary lending is limited by copyright laws, and it is quite expensive as currently practiced. One might argue that the practical effect of publication of scholarly journals by commercial publishers is a restriction of the dissemination of the works of academics — just the opposite of the best interest of those authors. Thus it appears that the relationship of the academic and the for-profit publisher no longer serves the best interest of both parties. Various solutions are being considered at many levels. It is important that information services librarians be involved and be viewed as involved in the resolution of this crucial problem. Above all, they must keep before all participants the imperative of access and preservation.

The concept of nonprofit discipline-specific full-text electronic databases accessible at cost offers the potential of speed and relative ease in the refereeing process, rapid availability of completed articles, and the widest possible dissemination of articles with the consent of authors whose drive to share their work could lead to the elimination of the current threat of copyright infringement. Such databases could prove particularly alluring to those disciplines where speed in sharing discoveries is of maximum importance. Within recent memory, the Center for Research Libraries considered the creation of a document delivery network for journal literature. Resolution of the resulting debate was that CRL has continued to build collections rather than a communication system.[8] It is possible that scholarly associations might join with CRL, OCLC, or similar organizations to develop article databases whose delivery would require not paper but a telecommunication system, perhaps that of OCLC which currently serves some libraries worldwide via a well-developed communications network. Other communications networks, like Bidnet, planned to link all the world's scholars, should also be examined.[9]

Commercial publishers, concerned by the possible loss of revenue, have developed in cooperation with library agencies, the ADONIS experiment designed to test the potential of journal article delivery on demand and thereby to gain income from "interlibrary lending" activities without additional costs to libraries. The project, to be completed in 1989, may provide useful guidance for large-scale document delivery.[10]

Were nonprofit or commercial electronic article databases available, librarians would not be so heavily burdened with the need to purchase, bind, store, and preserve the volume of journal literature which creates inordinate pressure on library budgets and space. Instead funds would be reallocated to provide access to needed literature for students, faculty, and others. Librarians would alert users to the databases and provide training needed for access. As well librarians would analyze and report on the real level of use made of the flood of scholarly output of recent years, much of which may have resulted from tenure and promotion pressures. Conceivably, such data, presently unavailable, might assist academe in the establishment of new priorities. And of particular concern, librarians would assure that these resources are made available to all who need them.

ACCESS AND PRESERVATION

Some believe that the resolution of the problem of access to needed information will be the demise of the library. Robert Hayes, however, has reminded us that libraries serve a role in society that no other institution seems to covet and that private enterprise is not likely to emulate. The traditional imperatives which Hayes insists are required of libraries include the provision of open availability of information provided by society or institutions free to individuals, and the preservation of the record. Information, he notes, has value to the individual and to society in the same sense as do medicine and law.[11] With the expansion of the volume of published material in most fields, the increasing interdisciplinary nature of scholarship, and the continuing increase in the costs of journals and books, researchers and other users are compelled to rely, perhaps more heavily than ever, on libraries to support basic information needs.[12] Worldwide more people than ever are engaged in scientific and scholarly activity assuring that the research record will grow. The results, part of the cycle of scholarship, are of enormous importance to mankind and should be shared with speed and efficiency.

DATABASE SEARCHING

Until recently the province of a few specially trained librarians, database searching has become basic to the provision of information services in today's library. Online services available now number several thousands. CD-ROM databases, recently added to libraries, are growing in available titles at a dizzying pace. Commercial publishers, alert to yet another marketing opportunity, are quickly making available disc versions of their printed and online reference products. Databases with no other counterpart are now distributed by both online and disc vendors. The Government Printing Office appears intent upon replacing a number of its print and microform services with CD-ROM. Librarians are pressed to learn to use, manage, and to judiciously evaluate databases in all versions with the same critical eye used for any other source. The goal should be to view each for its value in providing useful content to those in need based upon the repertoire of sources available. Until that experience has been gained librarians generally will be reluctant to cancel print versions of automated services.

The equipment for accessing local CD-ROM files is evolving from single disc microcomputer stations to multidisc access juke-boxes, with the possibility of providing multipoint access through bibliographic utilities on local mainframes, perhaps through online public access catalogs. Online vendors, determined to compete and perhaps to drive CD-ROM from the marketplace, have made nonprime time access available at attractive prices.[13] At least one has offered on an experimental basis unlimited searching for a flat fee.[14] The new services present a variety of search protocols. Until a few standardized protocols emerge, the provision of a variety of automated services results in confusion for end searchers. Of particular concern is the need to guide users through this period. Faculty may find the new technology particularly intimidating. Individuals or small group training sessions in subject areas of immediate interest can do much to relieve anxiety, especially among senior faculty.

Information services librarians must maintain all traditional services while adding new, automated, highly user-attractive services. At times they must work to convince patrons that automated databases may not serve an information need as well as one of the old print standbys. Physical housing requirements add to the headaches as traditional reference units, often suffering crowded conditions, must find space for new tools which also vie with more traditional sources for scarce collection development dollars. The impact on the use of local collections and on interlibrary loan must be followed closely as experience is gained with user access to direct database searching. Publishers, eager to provide those services most likely to lure sales, need and seek the advice of librarians. It is crucial that librarians, mindful of the information needs of clients, provide such guidance, even when it is not requested.

REFERENCE AND LIBRARY INSTRUCTION

The work of reference librarianship is, through added service and change brought on by automation, being transformed into information services librarianship. Tasks such as responding to reference needs, providing library use instruction, preparing bibliographies and other aids, verifying citations, and the selection of reference sources, continue in importance. They are supplemented by the transition from an emphasis on ownership to access, with new requirements for collection development, faculty liaison, and increasing demands in database searching. To date, improved access has been to bibliographic data, not generally to documents themselves. Expectations have been raised and all too often frustrated. Information services will continue to bear the brunt of that dissatisfaction until document delivery channels are improved. As telefacsimile transmission, viewed as an interim delivery mode by many, becomes widely utilized to hasten today's relatively slow interlibrary loan traffic, one can imagine the growth yet to be realized in that service.

In many libraries the range and level of responsibilities of information services librarians have become overwhelming. Today librarians search online databases for clients who earlier searched print sources for themselves. With the advent of CD-ROM and end user searching, librarians assume yet another teaching role. The range and number of automated services available will continue to grow. The online public access catalog, OCLC, vendor-specific files such as those provided by EBSCO and Faxon for serials, and a variety of full-text and numeric files create opportunities for service previously impossible; they also add to the demands made on staffs.

Formal bibliographic instruction programs, developed as a major services over the last decade, will continue to be important. They will smooth the introduction of new technologies and new source formats as well as introduce new services. The provision of training and guidance in the use of advanced subject literatures at the graduate and research levels will strengthen the claim of librarians to colleague status with the faculty.

As technology evolves, it is likely that bibliographic instruction will be offered in forums and formats quite different from today's lecture and tour. Local area networks may, for example, allow for what in effect could become long-térm continuous guidance through a research project or a dissertation. The opportunity and responsibility to create instruction suited to library users further defines the professional status of librarianship.

Library and university administrators must recognize the increased burden carried by reference librarians as their role broadens to include added information responsibilities. It should come as no surprise that these librarians may be less than sanguine about such matters, nor should the incidence of burnout experienced among them go unnoticed. Rather, close examination should be given to the degree to which reference personnel are subjected to burdensome work loads. While automation of technical service units reduced the need for professional librarians, its effective use mandates an increase in the number of workers who provide information services. Library management must encourage, not hinder, transitions which have become necessities if libraries are to fulfill the mission of the information age.

STAFF DEVELOPMENT

Skill in adapting to change and to the likelihood of an increase in the pace of change are attributes highly desirable in librarianship. Librarians trained in traditional libraries may experience dissonance in a constantly evolving environment. Sara Fine has pointed to the need for organizational and individual coping skills to handle debilitating stress.[15]

Those who accommodate well to evolving technology, software, communication modes, and information sources also will find it necessary to devote regular attention to training and study. Libraries must dedicate increased resources and attention to staff development through such avenues as peer training, professional activities, workshops, formal coursework and auditing courses, lectures, and informal discussion. Time provided in the work schedule for such efforts is a necessity. As well, librarians must recognize their own responsibility to allocate personal time and resources to gain and maintain competencies at needed levels. As professionals they must participate in, contribute to, and receive support from their colleagues.

CONCLUSIONS

As the sophisticated electronic databases used to control the bibliographic records of the world's publishing output have become increasingly complete and more widely dispersed, they have become amazingly easier to utilize. Access to them is available not only in libraries, but also in offices, laboratories, and in homes. The publishing explosion continues unabated as does the appetite of the world for the information it can identify more readily than ever before. Libraries can no longer appear as self-sufficient as they did prior to automation. Large-scale cooperation among libraries has served to fill reasonably, but by no means adequately, the growing demands on their resources. Computer technologies merged with communication modes have created the potential for the fulfillment of user demand for information. This environment compels the library world to rethink priorities and roles. It creates unparalleled opportunities for service and increased responsibilities for those who provide them. Today's information services librarian is challenged as never before by the demands of that mission. He/she must develop expertise in a subject along with a working knowledge of its bibliographic universe, become skilled in utilizing all sources relevant to that universe from the traditional to that most currently available. He/she will continue to build collections, but in a more limited fashion than in the past and based upon cooperative agreements with other libraries and information agencies. The provision of access to needed information and its preservation will become the major challenges of information services librarians over the next two decades.

NOTES

1. U.S. Congress. Office of Technology Assessment, *Technology and the American Economic Transition for the Future* (Washington, D. C.: U. S. Government Printing Office, May 1988) 3.

2. Julie M. Neway, *Information Specialist as Team Player in the Research Process* (Westport, CT: Greenwood Press, 1985) 152.

3. Nancy E. Gwinn and Paul H. Mosher, "Coordinated Collection Development: The RLG Conspectus," *College & Research Libraries 44 (March 1983): 129.*

4. Ibid., 133.

5. Anthony W. Ferguson, Joan Grant and Joel S. Rutstein, "The RLG Conspectus: Its Uses and Benefits," *College & Research Libraries 49 (May 1988): 204.*

6. Charles B. Osburn, "Collection Development: The Link Between Scholarship and Library Resources," in *Priorities for Academic Libraries* eds. Thomas J. Galvin and Beverly P. Lynch (San Francisco: Jossey-Bass, 1982), 51.

7. Peter Watson, "Collection Development and Evaluation Section (CODES)" *RASD UPDATE* 9 (April/June 1988): 16.

8. Scott Bennett, "Current Initiatives and Issues in Collection Management," *The Journal of Academic Librarianship* 10 (November 1984): 259.

9. Ken King, address, "The Scholar & His Information: A look at the 1990s," Preconference on Collection Development in the Electronic Age, Ameri-

can Library Association, Resources and Technical Services Division, New Orleans, 8 July 1988.

10. Robert M. Campbell and Barrie T. Stern, "ADONIS—A New Approach to Document Delivery," *Microcomputers for Information Management* 4 (June 1987): 87.

11. Robert M. Hayes, address, "Managing Scholarly Information: Implications & Strategies," Preconference Collection Development in the Electronic Age, American Library Association, Resources and Technical Services Division, New Orleans, 8 July 1988.

12. Robert M. Hayes, ed., *Universities, Information Technology, and Academic Libraries: The Next Twenty Years* (Norwood, NJ: Ablex Publishing Corporation, 1986), 41.

13. Martin Kesselman, "Online Update," *Wilson Library Bulletin* 62 (February 1988): 72-73.

14. "Library Patrons Beta Test Easynet 'Answer Machine'," *Information Today* 4 no. 10 (1988): 1.

15. Sara Fine, "Technologies and Libraries: A Behavioral Perspective," in *Community Information: Proceedings of the 43rd ASIS Annual Meeting*, eds. Alan R. Benenfeld and Edward J. Kazlauskas (White Plains, NY: Knowledge Industry Publications, 1980).

Allocation of Staff in the Academic Library: Relevant Issues and Consideration of a Rationale

Donald G. Frank

INTRODUCTION

Allocation of professional and classified staff in libraries is a complex, sensitive process. In academic libraries, expenditures for human resources total 54% of overall budgets.[1] Effective and efficient utilization of all staff is a primary requisite in the organization and delivery of quality bibliographic services to faculty and students. Assuming sufficient numbers of qualified personnel are available, they need to be assigned or allocated to appropriate bibliographic units within the library or library system. In the planning process, we strive to insure that the "right number of people with the right skills are available at the right time and place."[2]

The personnel function includes those activities related to recruitment, selection, training, development, and evaluation of employees. Too frequently, placement of staff is a neglected element. How are staff allocated in the college or university library setting and who is responsible for the decisions associated with the placement of staff? The achievement of organizational goals and objectives is dependent on the effective utilization of human resources. As budgetary constraints become more evident at institutions of higher education and as academic librarians attempt to provide first-rate bib-

---

Donald G. Frank is Head Science-Engineering Librarian at the University of Arizona.

liographic services for an increasingly sophisticated clientele, the necessity of effective staff utilization is accented.

In this paper, the concept of staff allocation will be explored from an organizational perspective. A rationale for the allocation of professional and classified staff is proposed and considered in relation to the strategic goals of the library. Since decisions on the allocation of staff are made within the context of a socio-political environment, relevant social and political factors are examined. These factors underscore the sensitive nature of the allocation process.

RELEVANCE OF THE POLITICAL ENVIRONMENT

In academic libraries, policy decisions are deliberated within a socio-political environment. While especially applicable for institutions in the public sector, these conditions exist for all academic libraries. Morrow describes politics as a struggle among competing forces for the right to control the character of public policy.[3] An important element of this definition is the term "struggle." The notion of a struggle implies that individuals with different objectives compete for limited resources. Perceived in such a way, political activity and potential conflict over limited physical and human resources are inevitable.

The administrator must be aware of the major participants in and the different vagaries of the general political environment. At the state level, colleges and universities compete for public revenues. After each educational institution receives its specific appropriation, the various academic departments and the library compete for needed financial resources. Hopefully, the director of libraries is able to secure necessary funding to support important bibliographic programs and services and to enhance the various collections. He or she is one of many academic administrators who express a calculated interest in the comprehensive allocation process.

After the overall library budget is determined and available for "rational" distribution, administrators within the library system participate in the process of allocation. At stake are essential physical and monetary resources. Negotiations are affected by the size and organization of the library and the internal values system. In the relatively small library, decisions in the allocation process are usually considered by a limited number of administrators or managers. Deliberations tend to be less politicized. As the size of the library increases, the nature of the political climate intensifies as more characters compete for needed resources. With sophisticated reference, online, and instructional services, comprehensive collection development, and an extensive technical services infrastructure, competition for all resources becomes intense. More administrators pursue necessary resources to support programs and services they perceive as important or essential. These individuals negotiate, cooperate, and compete as they attempt to justify a specific degree of support for particular bibliographic activities.

In large libraries or library systems, a considerable number of sophisticated and costly programs and services have been implemented over the past decade. An increasing emphasis is being placed on collection development and management, especially as acquisitions budgets are steadily eroded by inflationary pressures. In efforts to maintain online catalogs and other online systems, staff in technical services departments must cope with the details of complex and ever-changing automated operating procedures. As the "technology" of public and technical services becomes more complex and as additional programs and services are implemented to satisfy the bibliographic needs of users, all members of the staff feel increased pressure. Too frequently, optimal numbers of professional and classified staff are not available to assist in the delivery of these bibliographic services. With an increasing number of activities and duties being performed by an overworked staff, the concept of staff allocation becomes a relevant political issue. Competition over the allocation of human resources may surface as administrators attempt to obtain sufficient resources.

THE LITERATURE OF STAFF ALLOCATION

An examination of the literature concerned with the allocation of human resources in academic libraries reveals that few articles and reports have been published. Two articles focus on allocation of personnel in a technical services division of an academic library and in a system of public libraries, respectively.[4] Also, two reports discuss some of the rudimentary points associated with staff allocation in academic libraries.[5] These reports do not deal with allocation from an intellectual perspective. They are descriptive in nature. In addition, a considerable number of articles examine the concept of personnel allocation in institutions of higher education.[6] The majority of these articles are somewhat theoretical, characterized by the use of extensive mathematical or statistical formulae and models. Furthermore, several papers explore staff allocation in the private sector.[7]

In an examination of staff allocation for a technical services division, Heinritz develops a sequence of procedures to allocate available staff.[8] An "optimum allocation" is obtained through a series of calculations. The initial step involves the determination of the "per-volume processing time per full-time employee" for each department under consideration. To calculate these times, multiply the number of FTE employees in a department by the number of work hours in a selected time period; divide this result by the number of volumes processed in the selected period of time. For example, if there are 5.0 FTE employees in the Catalog Department who process 1,067 volumes over four weeks (160 work hours), then the per-volume processing time is $(5.0 \times 160)/1067$, or 3/4 hour.

Now, suppose that the per-volume processing time per full-time departmental employee is 1/3 hour for the Acquisitions Department, 3/4 hour for the Catalog Department, and 1/2 hour for the Serials Department. Also, suppose that there are 7.5 FTE employees in the Acquisitions Department, 5.0 in the Catalog Department, and 4.0 in the Serials Department. Divide each per-volume processing time by the corresponding number of FTE employees: $(1/3)/7.5 = 0.044$ hour of staff time required to process one volume in the Acquisitions Department; $(3/4)/5.0 = 0.150$ hour in the Catalog Department; and $(1/2)/4.0 = 0.125$ hour in the Serials Department. These numbers indicate that more staff time is required to process a volume in the Catalog Department. Heinritz concludes that staff should be transferred from the Acquisitions Department (lower number) to the Catalog Department (higher number). Accordingly, one reallocates staff from one department to another and, after an appropriate period of time, replicates the above calculations to assess progress toward the optimal staff allocation.

A second study of staff allocation, conducted by Little and

Saulmon, describes efforts to reallocate staff in a large public library system.[9] Over the years, staffing levels for branch libraries had been determined by various parameters, with a focus on circulation data. Also, local adaptations of guidelines recorded in *Minimum Standards for Public Libraries* (American Library Association) were employed. However, with increasing pressures from the immediate populace of users, several branch library directors pressed for additional staff.

As expected, the majority of branch library directors believed that their particular library either needed to retain all current staff or needed to add more staff. Consequently, an activity-oriented methodology was developed in an attempt to examine relative staff needs. Intensive deliberations defined relevant activities common to the different libraries. Then the times required to perform these activities were calculated or estimated for each library. As reference and other public services activities were difficult to measure, administrators decided that any staff time remaining after performing other defined activities would be recorded as time devoted to the reference activity.

After all relevant activities are identified and associated times are computed for each library, a series of calculations is employed to determine potential staff transfers. Primary variables in these calculations include: (a) staff time available at each library under current staffing levels to perform the identified activities; (b) staff times available for reference services after performing other duties. An arithmetic average of the number of staff hours available for reference services per hour is calculated for all branch libraries. This average becomes the level of equitable staffing for each library, within a tolerance of plus or minus one day (or 8 hours) of staff time per week. The variance from this average staff time availability per hour is then computed and used to determine whether or not a library should receive additional staff, lose staff, or remain unaffected. If the variance falls between -0.2 and $+0.2$ for a particular library, no staff changes are necessary for the library. Staff transfers are recommended when the variance from the average staff time available per hour for reference services is less than -0.2 or exceeds $+0.2$.

Allocation of staff in several British academic libraries is deliberated in a collection of papers published by the Council of Polytechnic Librarians.[10] With increasing demand for sophisticated bibliographic services and little or no increase in staff, administrators were concerned. In particular, overall activity for public and technical services divisions increased by approximately 50% at one of these libraries over a four-year period. Due to budgetary constraints, the number of available staff positions actually decreased over the same period of time.

In an attempt to cope with external pressures and overworked personnel, automated procedures were implemented to enhance efficiency of operations. Additionally, some staff hours were transferred from the Acquisitions and Catalog Departments to public services areas as a result of reductions in the acquisitions budget. As the pace of activity continued to escalate, all departmental administrators were asked to provide estimates on both current and future staff needs. In general, administrators believed that additional positions would be necessary to accomplish departmental goals, with significant staff increases requested by 11 public services administrators.

While this systematic approach did not eliminate existing staff problems, several notable outcomes were evident. First, administrators were pleased that they were asked to participate in the process. Second, all administrators requested additional professional and classified staff. Third, the staff transfers from technical to public services accented the need for individuals who were flexible in nature. Finally, administrators were considering possible reductions in programs and/or services as a result of continuing staff shortages.

Several studies on the allocation of academic and nonacademic staff in the general university environment have been conducted.[11] These studies are characterized by the application of statistical tests in the development of intricate models. Common variables used in the construction of the models include: staff time devoted to teaching undergraduate and graduate students; staff time devoted to research activities, including perceived value of and money generated by particular research projects; staff-student ratios; and time devoted to administrative and/or consultative activities.

Traditionally, academic staff allocations between departments are based on the teaching function, usually with the objective of arranging equitable teaching assignments. In these studies, considerable attention is devoted to the exercise of defining and enumerating the various tasks that comprise comprehensive research activities. Many of the relevant parameters and variables, statistical analyses, and associated models are not directly applicable to the academic library. Also, the models tend to be theoretical in nature. However, interested academic librarians should note the overall approach, with a focus on the identification of important variables and the potential use of appropriate statistical tests.

TOWARD A NORMATIVE THEORY OF STAFF ALLOCATION

Allocation of personnel in academic libraries is a critical concept. If the right people are in the right place, organizational effectiveness will be enhanced. The intent of this statement is accented when administrators are forced to provide bibliographic programs and services with perceived staff shortages.

Few papers have been published on staff allocation. In the previously discussed papers by Heinritz and Little/Saulmon, procedures to attain equitable staff allocation through various arithmetic calculations are described. These are estimable attempts to derive rational methodologies for personnel allocation in particular library settings. Nevertheless, important differences in the utilization and efficiency of employees as individuals and as participants in groups are not considered. Also, differences in the actual flow of work in distinct departments or units are not deliberated. Additional efforts are necessary to examine the overall context in which the process of staff allocation occurs in an attempt to establish a viable rationale for appropriate and necessary decisions.

In *The Library in the University*, Higham enumerates two principles on general staff utilization. First, a "library should employ no more staff than are necessary to enable it to carry out its task."[12] Second, an "inadequately staffed library progressively lowers its service level."[13] Elaborating on these statements, Higham asserts that

> there is a right level of staffing which we should neither fall short of nor exceed. The difficulty is to identify the level in terms of how many staff carrying out what duties. A new library will appoint a small team comprising the minimum number to carry out the tasks which exist at the start, and add to that number as the system expands, creating new small teams within the original structure. Older libraries have simply been doing this for a longer time, but the longer it is done, the greater the danger of losing sight of the original structure and creating a lack of balance.[14]

What is the "right level" of staffing? How is this level related to the performance of duties in different units within the library? In a sense, Higham's statements focus on the relationship between staff utilization and organizational effectiveness and underscore the importance of personnel allocation. While the concept of staff allocation is not explained or developed by Higham, the points and questions raised by his succinct comments are noteworthy as they probe the surface of allocation theory.

Allocation of staff needs to be considered as a process that occurs within a political environment. In such an environment, on what basis are decisions made to allocate staff to one activity or department over another activity or department? It is a rare occasion, if ever, when administrators claim that they have sufficient staff to attain necessary and desirable goals. In general, human resources are perceived as limited at many academic libraries. If so, the rationale on which human resources are allocated should be a topic of concern to all administrators.

In the consideration or development of a rationale for staff allocation, what are the relevant parameters that should be deliberated to determine the actual allocation of human resources? Or, what decisions need to be made to determine the allocation of staff to a specific activity or a particular unit within the library? First, the strategic goals of the library should reflect the comprehensive goals of the college or university in terms of overall direction and academic emphasis. Changes in academic programs and priorities usually occur methodically, but may accelerate during times of administrative change or financial crisis at the institutional or state level. If senior academic officials perceive "Research I" status as desirable, for example, the institutional emphasis on science and technology will increase. If this occurs, in theory, administrators in the library will allocate or reallocate additional physical and human resources to programs and services that support the scientific and technical disciplines. In reality, such an allocation is possible over a period of time only after administrators deliberate sensitive and difficult issues within the political environment.

Relative priorities attached to primary activities, programs, and services constitute a second allocation parameter. As noted above, the cumulative aggregation of these priorities should reflect the overall direction of the college or university. At the same time, priorities in different units of the library should be related to staffing patterns in the units and the library. As current activities are examined and emerging trends are contemplated, priorities associated with these activities and trends need to be continually examined in light of anticipated staff needs. Too frequently, academic librarians scrutinize activities and programs from a perspective that is more egalitarian than evaluative. A critical approach is necessary to enhance the quality of decisions on the relative importance of major activities. After priorities are established, the necessary internal staff allocations or reallocations can be deliberated.

The flow of work within departments and in the library is another relevant parameter on which decisions to allocate staff may be based. A critical factor is efficiency of operations. Increased efficiency might minimize the need for staff in a particular unit or area. For example, implementation and utilization of automated procedures will affect the flow of work. In theory, efficiency will be enhanced, especially in units of technical services where procedures tend to be repetitive. When this is the case, staff may be reallocated within technical services or from technical services to perceived understaffed public services departments.

Additionally, the flow of work may be affected by decisions external to the library. If the acquisitions budget is decreasing relative to inflationary pressures, for example, the number of bibliographic materials purchased will decline. As a result, the number of monographs and serials to be processed will decrease, affecting the flow of work. Again, questions on the use of staff should be discussed to determine if current allocations are appropriate to equitable.

In the "Standards for College Libraries," professional staff guidelines are proposed.[15] Specifically, the "staff should be of adequate size and quality to meet the library's needs for services, programs, and collection organization."[16] A formula, based on enrollment and collection size, is used to compute the number of "required" librarians. In a similar process, another formula is used in this calculation for university libraries.[17] These standards and guidelines provide a measure of perspective for the academic library. In particular, the standards serve as targets for those libraries considered to be understaffed and can be employed by the Director of Libraries in attempts to gain additional staff for the library or library system. Accordingly, they constitute a relevant parameter on which decisions to allocate staff to the library might be based and should be emphasized by the Director of Libraries in negotiations with other university administrators.

CONCLUDING COMMENTS

Allocation of professional and classified staff is a sensitive issue that takes place within a political environment. It is a process that occurs directly or indirectly, depending on administrative attitude, current staffing needs and patterns, and financial conditions. Allocation is an important process as effective staff allocation will enhance organizational effectiveness.

According to the ACRL Committee on Performance Measures, "academic libraries . . . need to decide what services are important."[18] To arrive at such a decision, serious deliberations must take place to determine relevant strategic goals and associated priorities. Determination of goals and priorities is the initial phase in the process of staff allocation.

In the academic setting, some administrators may not feel comfortable deliberating staff allocation. A sense of competition may surface and possibly intensify on occasion. Generally, if professional librarians and classified staff are perceived as position-flexible within the particular library, discussions and eventual decisions on allocation will occur in an administrative climate that is more conducive to organizational change.

A rationale for staff allocation needs to be refined. On what basis should staff be allocated to a particular activity? This is a critical question that deserves additional attention in academic library research.

REFERENCES

1. Robert E. Molyneux, "Staffing Patterns and Library Growth at ARL Libraries, 1962/63 to 1983/84," *Journal of Academic Librarianship,* 12 (November 1986): 292-297.
2. Robert Sergean, *Librarianship and Information Work: Job Characteristics and Staffing Needs* (London: The British Library, Research and Development Reports, 1977), p. 2.
3. William L. Morrow, *Public Administration: Politics, Policy, and the Political System* (New York: Random House, 1980), p. 3.
4. Fred J. Heinritz, "Optimum Allocation of Technical Services Personnel," *Library Resources and Technical Services,* 13 (winter 1969): 99-101; Paul L. Little and Sharon A. Saulmon, "Realistic Allocation of Branch Library Staff," *Library Journal,* 104 (February 1, 1979): 356-358.
5. See the Newcastle and Middlesex reports in: Council of Polytechnic Librarians, *Working Papers on . . . Allocation of Staff* (London: British Library Board, British Library R & D Report No. 5773, 1983).
6. For example, see R. Ball, "Allocation of Academic Staff in Universities," *Higher Education,* 9 (July 1980): 419-427; Frank G. Dijkman, "An Allocation Model for Teaching and Nonteaching Staff in a Decentralized Institution," *Research in Higher Education,* 22 (1): 3-18; E. H. Broekhuizen and J. G. Frankfort, "An Allocation Model for Non-Academic Staff," *International Journal of Institutional Management in Higher Education,* 5 (July 1981): 123-133; Stephen Griew, "A Model for the Allocation of Academic Staff Resources," *Canadian Journal of Higher Education,* 10 (2): 73-84.
7. For example, see Tugrul Aladag, "A Probabilistic Approach to Staff Allocation," *Business Economics,* 14 (January 1979): 32-37.
8. Fred J. Heinritz, "Optimum Allocation," pp. 99-101.
9. Paul L. Little and Sharon A. Saulmon, "Realistic Allocation," pp. 356-358.
10. Council of Polytechnic Librarians, *Working Papers on . . . Allocation of Staff* (no pagination).
11. R. Ball, "Allocation of Academic Staff," pp. 419-427; Frank G. Dijkman, "An Allocation Model," pp. 3-18; E. H. Broekhuizen and J. G. Frankfort, "An Allocation Model," pp. 123-133; Stephen Griew, "A Model," pp. 73-84.

12. Norman Higham, *The Library in the University: Observations on a Service* (Boulder, CO: Westview Press, 1980), p. 140.
13. Ibid., p. 140.
14. Ibid., p. 140.
15. American Library Association, Association of College and Research Libraries, College Standards Committee, "Standards for College Libraries, 1986," *College and University Libraries News*, 47 (March 1986): 189-200.
16. Ibid., p. 194.
17. American Library Association, Association of College and Research Libraries, and Association of Research Libraries, Joint ARL-ACRL Committee on University Library Standards, "Standards for University Libraries," *College and University Libraries News*, 40 (April 1979): 101-110.
18. Judith Axler Turner, "Academic Libraries Urged to Study Needs of Users and Set Performance Standards," *Chronicle of Higher Education*, 34 (January 27, 1988): 2.

Creating A New Classification System for Technical and Supervisory Library Support Staff

Lucy R. Cohen

INTRODUCTION

In 1984, the University of Michigan Library Personnel Office conducted a review of all nonlibrarian professional support staff, 80 out of the approximately 350 regular full-time staff positions. These 80 positions are part of the University's overall Professional and Administrative (P&A) job family.

The University of Michigan P&A classification structure includes 20 salary grades. A review of the University's supervisory titles and salary grades revealed that approximately 46 different titles existed. Of the 49, one title was classified in the 03 salary grade, 3 titles were classified in the 04 salary grade, and the rest were classified in the 05 grade or higher. In contrast all of the Library's supervisory staff (23 Library Supervisors) were classified within one title and salary grade, 04. In addition, University technical and research staff were classified broadly and within all of the P&A ranges. All of the Library's technical staff members (45 Technical Library Assistants) were classified into one title and salary grade, 03. Therefore, prior to the study, 85% of the Library P&A staff were squeezed into two classification titles and salary grades. The remaining 15% were either classified as Administrative Assistants (grade 04), or scattered as specialists within the 07 and 08 salary grades.

It became evident from reviewing vacancy announcements and reclassification requests that the role of the Library P&A staff mem-

---

Lucy R. Cohen is Manager, Personnel and Payroll at the University of Michigan Library.

© 1989 by The Haworth Press, Inc. All rights reserved.

bers had evolved and changed as responsibilities shifted in response to the changing role of the professional librarian. As professional librarians started to focus on resolving complex policy and standards questions, plan for new technology, provide increasingly more research assistance to faculty and students, participate in outreach programs and administrative projects, and involve themselves in long-range planning with greater budgeting and personnel administration dues, they increasingly relinquished responsibilities to their P&A staff members.

P&A staff were performing original cataloging, independently supervising branch libraries, managing several units within a large divisional library, solving problems related to the physical maintenance of the collection and buildings, and providing reference assistance to faculty and students including conducting data base searches.

Although the classification system prior to the study allowed for some movement from the 03 to the 04 salary grade, it did not allow for recognition between the different levels of technical work or supervisory and management responsibilities.

To remedy the obvious inequities, the Library submitted a proposal to the University Personnel Office requesting that all Library P&A staff members' position descriptions be reviewed in a special classification study. The intent of this study was to closely examine the duties and responsibilities of the Library's P&A staff in order to insure that changes in assignments with the Library were appropriately recognized and that Library P&A positions were properly classified in relation to all University P&A positions.

THE CLASSIFICATION STUDY

The proposal submitted by the Library to the University Personnel Office outlined a plan to complete the study in four phases:

1. Definition of goals and development of data-gathering instruments;
2. Data gathering;
3. Data analysis; and
4. Implementation of the results.

Chart 1 outlines the timeline for the implementation of the study. The study began in January 1984 and targeted July 1, 1984 as the effective date for any classification changes. The July completion date was chosen because it is the start of the University's fiscal year. The first two months of the study were devoted primarily to discussions with the University Personnel Office staff about the goals of the study, the development of the data-gathering instruments, and the preparation of Library staff for the study. The actual data gathering occurred within a one-month time period, while data analysis lasted two months. Approximately one month was needed to implement the recommendations.

Phase 1 — Defining Goals and Developing the Data-Gathering Instrument

The goal of this study was to obtain accurate and descriptive information about the job duties performed by Library P&A staff members and to identify the levels of skills, ability and experience necessary to perform these responsibilities at the entry level. A memo to all P&A staff members and their supervisors was sent articulating this goal and emphasizing that the study was not intended to be an evaluation of a staff member's work. Staff members were also assured that if any reclassification downward occurred, it would not result in loss of wages. Additional information about the

CHART 1
UNIVERSITY OF MICHIGAN LIBRARY
CLASSIFICATION STUDY TIMELINE

ACTIVITIES	JAN	FEB	MAR	APR	MAY	JUN
Review of Proposal by University Personnel	___					
Library and University Personnel Develop Data Gathering Instrument		_____				
Data Gathering			___			
Data Analysis & Completion of Study				_____		
Implementation of Recommendations						___

study included that an appeal process would be available, that a moratorium on P&A reclassification would be in effect until the study was completed and the results implemented, and that the effective date for implementation of the results and any classification changes would be July 1, 1984.

During discussions with the University Personnel Staff it was agreed that the Library Personnel Office would develop a Position Analysis Questionnaire (see Appendix A). The intent of the questionnaire was to obtain the following information:

— the task being performed;
— the knowledge requirements (education, experience, skills) to perform the tasks;
— how the knowledge applied in problem-solving and decision-making responsibilities;
— the impact a position had on the library, the university, and the profession;
— the amount of independence a staff member had in performing his/her responsibilities;
— the amount and type of accountability required of the staff member;
— the supervisory responsibilities exercised (number of staff supervised and the kind of supervision required); and
— the types of tasks performed by subordinate staff members.

In addition to the Position Analysis Questionnaire (PAQ), Library Personnel agreed to gather manning and process charts, as needed. Examples of manning charts were unit and divisional organizational charts. Examples of process charts were workflow charts and input/output analysis.

It became very clear that the most important part of this study was to describe the work being performed at the Library to University Personnel staff members and to educate them about the complexities of library tasks and the breadth of responsibilities inherent in technical and supervisory positions. Prior experience with the University Personnel Office indicated that library work was not always well understood or valued.

Phase 2—Data Gathering

The PAQs were mailed to affected staff members and their supervisors with a cover memo inviting them to training sessions, each one limited to 20 participants. These training sessions were instrumental to our receiving accurate, clear, and comparable information. In addition the sessions provided Library Personnel with an additional opportunity to review the goals of the study and highlight the "rules." They allowed staff the opportunities to ask questions and to review the PAQs, alleviating stress and concerns about possible negative outcomes of the study for individual employees. Staff members were encouraged to continue to ask questions as they filled out the PAQs.

Phase 3—Evaluation of Data

The first review of the data gathered was conducted by Library Personnel. The PAQs were read carefully and sorted by four distinct skill categories: Supervisory, Technical, Administrative, and Special Skills.

The supervisory category included 37 staff members who were responsible for supervision of staff, workflow, collections and/or building facilities. The technical group consisted of 32 staff members who were responsible for copy and original cataloging, inputting and converting records and bibliographic and data base searching. The administrative grouping included eight staff members who had budgetary responsibilities and provided administrative support. The fourth category consisted of three staff members who had special skills and "one-of-a-kind" positions such as the Document Restorer, the Head of Photoduplication and the Head of Bindery Preparation and Microfilming.

The PAQs were copied and forwarded to the University Personnel Office in the four categories. Library Personnel then arranged for University Personnel staff members to receive demonstrations of the Library's computerized systems, RLIN, GEAC, and INNOVACQ. As the University Personnel staff reviewed and analysed the PAQs, Library Personnel responded immediately to questions asked, often inviting them to visit departments, check on projects, files, records, materials, and workflow. Library Personnel forwarded manning and process charts and provided additional information on unit sizes, circulation statistics and collection sizes. Most importantly Library Personnel staff spent many hours explaining the complexities of library work and its impact on faculty, students, and the profession in general.

The analysis of the technical skills category was conducted using a task analysis approach (Appendix B), while the analysis of the supervisory category was conducted using a systematic approach based on staff size, complexity and variety of tasks performed by the subordinate staff, and how independent the supervisor performed his/her responsibilities.

Upon completion of these analyses, Library Personnel and University Personnel jointly conducted a second sort of the PAQs. As a result, the levels within each category were refined and compared with other University positions. The office staffs jointly developed classification descriptions for levels within the four skills categories. Recommendations submitted to the University's Compensation Office included general definitions for each skills category in addition to points assigned to each level within the categories. The assigned points were used to determine appropriate salary grades after a final audit for each level was completed by University Personnel. The Library's P&A staff members were placed in appropriate classification after a final sort was conducted by both Library and University Personnel staff.

Phase 4 – Implementation of the Results

The final results of this study were very gratifying. The review verified that P&A were performing higher-level technical and managerial functions than their previous classification indicated. In order to compensate for the higher-level functions and maintain equity within the University Classification System for P&A staff, four new classification descriptions were written and the existing two – Technical Library Assistant and Library Supervisor – were rewritten and renamed to fit the new system. The Administrative Assistant classifications and the three specialist positions remained unchanged.

More than one third (37.5%) of the P&A staff were reclassified with upward salary adjustments, 32.5% moved up one salary grade, 5% moved up two salary grades. A few positions were identified for downward reclassification after the incumbent left the position. This identification remains confidential and is used for the purpose of position control only. As promised at the beginning of the study, no staff member suffered any losses in wages due to the review.

The four new classification descriptions and two rewritten existing descriptions define three levels within each of the technical and supervisory category:

> Technical Library Assistant (TLA) I, II, II
> Library Supervisor I (SUPR I), Coordinator of Technical Operations (CTO) and Library Supervisor II (SUPR II).

While previously 85% of the P&A staff were compressed within two titles and two salary grades, their positions are now disbursed within six titles and four salary grades (see Chart 2).

An added benefit of the new system was additional upward mobility for Library staff members. The Coordinator of Technical Operations (CTO) level provides the link between technical and supervisory categories. Library staff members can be promoted to the 05 salary grade with either technical or supervisory experience or knowledge.

CONCLUSION

The result of the study has proven very effective over the last four years in maintaining equitable compensation levels for Library P&A staff members. Reclassification requests and new position de-

CHART 2
UNIVERSITY OF MICHIGAN LIBRARY
NEW SALARY GRADES FOR P&A POSITIONS

Salary Grades:	P&A 03	P&A 04	P&A 05	P&A 06
Job Titles	TLA I	TLA II	TLA III	
		SUPR I	CTO	SUPR II

scriptions are easily reviewed and appropriately classified. As can be expected, however, the system's effectiveness will diminish with time as library positions change because of new technology and new programs.

APPENDICES

APPENDIX A

UNIVERSITY OF MICHIGAN LIBRARY
POSITION DESCRIPTION QUESTIONNAIRE
Professional and Administrative Positions

Position Data

Name_____

Current Job Classification Title_____

Division_____Section_____

Unit_____

Work Address_____Work Phone_____

Immediate Supervisor (person to whom you report)_____

Supervisor's Title_____ Supervisor's Phone_____

APPENDIX A (continued)

Introduction

The purpose of this study is to obtain accurate and descriptive information about the job duties currently being performed by Library P & A staff members and to identify the levels of skills, ability, and experience necessary to perform these responsibilities at the entry level.

The information obtained will be used to update classification descriptions and to determine if any Library P & A positions are inappropriately classified within the University system. This questionnaire will not be used to evaluate performance.

Instructions

1. Please look over the entire questionnaire before you begin. Each question should be answered completely and accurately. If a question is not applicable, please write "N/A".

2. In filling out the questionnaire, please print legibly in black ink or type.

3. If you have any problems in filling out the questionnaire, please contact _____.

4. If you wish to make additional comments regarding your position, please use page --- of this questionnaire. Please feel free to attach any other information you feel would be useful in describing your position.

5. Please complete the questionnaire and return it to your supervisor. Your supervisor will review the questionnaire and add any comments or clarifications in the Supervisor's Comments Section. Completed questionnaires should be returned to the Library Personnel Office by ---------.

Position Duties

1. Summarize your basic position function in one short statement.

   Examples:

   * Supervises the operations of the Medical Library's Circulation Department.

   * Performs simple to moderately complex original cataloging of monographs.

   * Supervises the activities of the Library Payroll Office.

   * Coordinates the pre-catalog searching, card production and filing within Technical Services and the Public Catalog.

APPENDIX A (continued)

2. Briefly describe the specific recurring duties which you perform in the normal course of your work. List the duties in order of their importance and indicate the average percent of time applied to each duty over the course of a year. In describing your duties, begin each phrase with a word denoting action. Be specific...avoid generalities such as "attend meetings", "manage people", "prepare paperwork". You may find it helpful to organize your answer on a separate sheet before completing this question. See next page for examples.

Examples of Recurring Duties

Duties	% of Time Applied Over a Year
* Plans, organizes, and develops training materials for support staff.	25%
* Resolves complex serials problems.	10%
* Identifies and corrects or refers for correction cataloging and recording problems.	40%
* Hires, trains, and revises the work of part-time employees.	50%
* Maintains the course reserve collection for the Fine Arts Library.	15%
* Assigns classification numbers.	25%

Duties (In Order of Importance)	% of Time Applied Over a Year
	100%

3. What special knowledge, experience, and/or skills are <u>required</u> for successful performance of your job duties? (Please check the appropriate lines.)

* Knowledge of foreign language(s) ____

   Specific language(s) required: _____

* Experience in searching data bases (DIALOG, etc.) ____

* Experience with library automation:

   Which systems? GEAC____   OCLC____   INNOVACQ____

   RLIN____   OTHER____(specify)_____

APPENDIX A (continued)

What kind of experience?   Searching only   ----
                           Inputting/editing   ----
                           Training other users   ----
                           Systems implementation ----

* Experience with other equipment (e.g., keypunch, photoduplication, etc.)
  ---- Specify equipment: _____

* Supervisory experience ----

* Accounting/bookkeeping skills ----

* Knowledge of the card catalog:

Which catalog(s)? Public catalog ----   Divisional library catalog ----

What kind(s) of   Searching ----   Training others to search ----
catalog use?   Filing   ----   Training others to file   ----

* Knowledge of bibliographic tools (which?):

  National Union Catalogs   ----
  Union List of Serials, New Serials Titles   ----
  Library of Congress Subject Headings   ----
  Classification Schedules   ----
  Cutter tables   ----
  Other (Specify)

72

* Knowledge of particular categories of materials (which?):

    Government documents ----   Maps ----
    Microforms ----   Rare books/manuscripts ----
    Serials ----
    Other (specify) ---------------------------------------

* Other special knowledge, experience, and/or skills (please specify) ----
  ----
  ----

4. Does your job assignment include: Yes   No

   Setting your individual work priorities?   ----   ----
   Establishing procedures for your own work?   ----   ----

5. In what way(s) are you involved in a) setting unit priorities, b) establishing unit procedures, and/or c) establishing unit policies? Please mark only one in each column.

	(a) unit priorities	(b) unit procedures	(c) unit policies
Discussing/reviewing with immediate supervisor	----	----	----
Advising/providing input to immediate superv.	----	----	----

APPENDIX A (continued)

For each area (a) (b) and (c) above, please give specific examples of your involvement over the course of the past year.

----

6. In what way are you involved in the preparation of your unit's annual planning document?

Discussing/reviewing the document ----
Advising in the preparation ----
Developing a section of the document ----

7. Does your immediate supervisor: <u>Yes</u> <u>No</u>

Work outside your primary work area or department? ---- ----
Regularly work a shift different from you own? ---- ----

If you answered "yes" to either question above, please describe briefly the outside location and/or difference in shift.

----

8. Check the one item below which most nearly describes the amount of supervision your position normally receives:

Most or all work is done under close supervision, with frequent review of both the results of the work and the manner in which the work is performed. ____

Some work done under close supervision; most work done under general supervision with minimal emphasis on manner of performance, but close attention to results in terms of quality and quantity. ____

No work done under immediate supervision; most work done independently, with only occasional direction, and reviewed primarily on the basis of results. ____

Work done only under general direction, with emphasis on independence of method, and with accountability only for results. ____

Supervisory Duties

Questions 9 - 13 concern the amount and kind of supervision of other employees your position requires you to exercise. Please complete this section only if you have supervisory responsibilities (such as those described in number 9 below) for regular and/or temporary/hourly employees. If you have No supervisory duties, please mark the line below and skip to the next section.

My position does not include supervision of other employees. ____

75

APPENDIX A (continued)

9. Check each phrase that describes the kind of supervision you provide. Mark the appropriate column or columns to indicate the type(s) of employee supervised AND whether the employees supervised report to you <u>directly</u> or through others <u>(indirectly)</u>.

	REGULAR		TEMPORARY/HOURLY	
	Directly	Indirectly	Directly	Indirectly
Assign work, supervise workflow	----	----	----	----
Train and instruct	----	----	----	----
Answer questions	----	----	----	----
Revise work; check work for conformance to standards	----	----	----	----
Interview; provide hiring recommendations	----	----	----	----
Make final decision on hiring	----	----	----	----
Provide input on performance to other supervisors	----	----	----	----
Counsel and/or discipline unsatisfactory staff members	----	----	----	----
Provide recommendations for termination	----	----	----	----
Make final decision for termination	----	----	----	----

10. For each type of employee you supervise (regular or temporary/hourly, please fill in: (1) the <u>number of people</u> who report to you directly, and the number who report to you through others (indirectly), and (2) the <u>number of FTE</u> (full-time equivalents) who report to you, directly and indirectly. Enter a zero if you supervise no employees in a given category.

	REGULAR		TEMPORARY/HOURLY	
	Directly	Indirectly	Directly	Indirectly
1. Number of <u>people</u> supervised	----	----	----	----
2. Number of <u>FTE</u> supervised	----	----	----	----

11. What percentage of your time is spent supervising people? _____ %

12. Do any of the employees you supervise <u>directly</u> work outside your immediate work area or department? Yes --- No ---

If you answered "yes" above, please describe briefly the outside location <u>and</u> the employee(s) involved.

----

13. In this part, please list the classification(s) of the employees you supervise <u>directly</u>. Indicate the number of employees you supervise within each classification, and briefly summarize the employee's job duties. <u>Be specific</u>: if you supervise two employees in the same classification, but with different job duties, please describe the different jobs. Continue on next page if necessary.

77

APPENDIX A (continued)

Examples:

NUMBER	CLASSIFICATION	JOB DUTIES
2	Library Circulation Assistant I	Work at Circulation Desk: check materials in and out, process holds, calculate and collect fines, solve routine problems.
4	Student Assistants	Staff the Information Desk: answer patron questions (in person & on telephone): give directions; assist patrons in use of card catalog, Union List, etc.

NUMBER	CLASSIFICATION	JOB DUTIES

---

14. Describe the frequency and purpose of the contacts your position requires you to make with others outside your primary work unit. If there is more than one level within a category, please check the appropriate level(s).

Examples:

CATEGORY/LEVEL	FREQUENCY	PURPOSE
Library Staff		
Clerical ---	Daily	Answer Questions
Public ---	4 times/year	Get course reserve list

CATEGORY/LEVEL	FREQUENCY	PURPOSE
Library Staff		
Clerical ___		
Technical Library Assistants ___		
Supervisors ___		
Librarians ___		
Unit Heads ___		
Administrators ___		
Public		
Faculty ___		
Students ___		
Other (specify) ___		

APPENDIX A (continued)

Vendors _____

CATAGORY/LEVEL   FREQUENCY   PURPOSE

University Departments

   Staff   ___

   Supervisors   ___

   Administrators   ___

   Other (specify) ___

_____

Other (specify)

General Comments

15. Since no single questionnaire can cover every aspect of a job, we encourage you to use this space to list any additional comments describing your position or any additional comments in general.

Employee's Signature_____Date_____

When you have completed this questionnaire, please forward it to your supervisor.

Thank you for your cooperation.

APPENDIX A (continued)

SUPERVISOR'S COMMENT SECTION

It is important that you, the supervisor, review the questionnaire, since you may have a different perspective of the position being described. (For example, a person holding a position may tend to describe his or her own qualifications rather than the minimum qualifications required by the position.) DO NOT CHANGE THE INCUMBENT'S DESCRIPTION OF THE POSITION, but list your comments with reference to the appropriate question number in the incumbent's description. Please remember that this questionnaire is intended solely for the purpose of accurately describing the position in question. The information provided on the previous pages is not to be used for purposes of evaluating this indivdual's performance nor should your comments be addressed to this person.

Question Number	Comment(s)
----------	--
----------	--
----------	--
----------	--
----------	--
----------	--
----------	--

_____

_____

_____

_____

_____

_____

_____

____ I agree with the incumbent's position description as written.

____ I have discussed the above modification(s) with the incumbent and the incumbent agrees with the modification(s).

____ I have discussed the above modification(s) with the incumbent and the incumbent disagrees with the modification(s).

Please return the questionnaire to the Library Personnel Office, 404 Hatcher Graduate Library by _____.

Supervisor's Signature _____Date_____

APPENDIX B

LIBRARY TASK ANALYSIS

SUB I

Precat searching
RLIN searching
RLIN inputting
Card typing
GEAC inputting
Buhr conversion GEAC
Post-cataloging searching

LEVEL I

Transfers, withdrawals, reinstatements
Indexing of divisional backlogs
Training GEAC inputting
Revising call numbers
Buhr conversion RLIN
800 shelflist, modifying
Labadie copy cataloging
Modifying LC or member library records
Labelling
Public catalog card filing
Retrospective conversion inputting and
    editing records
Retrospective microform cataloging
Transcription cataloging
Managed backlog analysis
Record conversion into SPIRES
Verification of subject headings
<u>Edit</u> descriptive copy

LEVEL II	LEVEL III
Copy cataloging, music scores, books, serials	Slavic subject analysis (includes copy cataloging of books and serials)
Copy cataloging, rare books, STC project	Slavic classification (includes copy cataloging of books and serials)
Pre-cat searching, rare books, STC project	Brief record cataloging (original)
Retrospective conversion, <u>creating records</u>	Original cataloging
Serials copy cataloging	Original cataloging of sound recordings
Creates descriptive cataloging copy	
Authority work, creating cross references, links and name changes	
Cataloging card changes and corrections	
Training RLIN searching	
Training RLIN inputting	
Coordinating RLIN inputting	
Original cataloging of dissertations, theses, vertical files	

Training for Change: Staff Development in a New Age

Anne Grodzins Lipow

STAFF DEVELOPMENT AND ORGANIZATIONAL CHANGE

Staff is the most important resource in any library: they constitute the largest portion of a library's budget, they deliver the library's services, they operate the library's equipment, they shape the library's image. That is not new. What is new in any library is the pace of change: in the last 10 or so years our occupation — the tools we use to accomplish our mission, the mission itself, and even the patrons we serve — has been changing at a rate faster than it has changed in all previous decades combined; and there is no let-up in sight. Just about any issue of a library journal you pick up these days contains an article about organizational change — what causes it, what its components are, how to cope with it, how to manage it, who the players in it are, why some people resist it and how to deal with them, or how-my-library-dealt-with-it-good. Underlying each of the articles in the observation, explicit or implied, that something has changed about change in libraries. The articles focus on the concern of how staff could fare better through this inevitably unsettling era. The authors urge greater and better attention to the reeducation and retraining of all levels of library personnel to ensure the continuing effectiveness of the library. In other words, they call for more staff development.

Iowa University Library Director Sheila Creth, responding to the question "In your opinion, what is the number one personnel issue

---

Anne Grodzins Lipow is Director of Library Instructional Services at the University of California, Berkeley.

in academic libraries today?" described the relationship between staff development and change:

> The magnitude and scope of change that now exists in most libraries suggests that we must . . . devote greater resources to staff development than we have in the past . . . Administrators need to make a commitment to staff development . . . to insure that staff have the knowledge and abilities to work effectively in the rapidly changing and very demanding environment. Library administrators cannot expect that . . . experienced staff will always make the transition to a new environment with different responsibilities without considerable attention to their learning needs.[1]

By contrast, the number one personnel issue in past years was not staff development, but rather, depending on the particular decade, recruitment and retention, motivation, conflict resolution, affirmative action, salaries.

Staff development, then, is regarded as an important vehicle for using existing personnel resources to implement more change faster and better. Without staff development, libraries have to accomplish change by hiring new personnel with the needed new skills and waiting till the "dead wood" leaves. If staff development is a key answer to our current problems, why don't we take it more seriously? What do we know about how it works?

STAFF DEVELOPMENT EDUCATION VS. TRAINING

There is, according to learning specialists, a difference between education and training: education enhances awareness, knowledge and understanding; training seeks to change behavior. Also, there is a difference between education and reeducation, and between training and retraining. Reeducation requires the student to abandon concepts that once were true but no longer are; retraining requires the student to UNlearn what used to be a competency but no longer is. Libraries have long offered, to one degree or another, staff development programs that address both the educational and training needs of their staffs, but the programs have been and still are relatively vague and informal. Sending someone off to a workshop on "managing stress" or demonstrating to staff new forms of information storage, or requiring attendance at an ad hoc program that deals with a particular crisis are all considered "staff development" activities. If we are to pin our success in the fast-paced world of the "information age" on staff development, we had better become more serious, less vague, and more formal about it; we should know what we want out of it and how to get it.

CURRENT TRAINING PROGRAMS IN LIBRARIES

Our efforts to become more serious about staff development can be demonstrated by a shift away from purely educational programs in libraries. In recent years they have taken on a new importance as the *behaviors* of library personnel—not just their knowledge or their attitudes—need to change to keep up with rapid and extensive change in the organization. It is no longer possible to assume that library school training will remain valid for very long. It is likely, too, that training given to support staff during the first year of any five-year period would be obsolete by the end of the five years.

When change was slower in the library, there was plenty of time to train someone to do a job, and once done, there was only occasional need to update skills. "Staff development" programs were mostly voluntary, and for the most part were of the "consciousness raising" or educational variety. Staff development programs gave the participant some time away from the job to learn about the "big picture," even to learn a particular skill, but rarely was there any expectation that what was learned had to be used on the job. Often, supervisors of the participants were unaware of what they were sending their staff off to learn and had no expectations about what might go differently after the participant returned to work.

Two ARL SPEC Flyers introducing SPEC Kits on "Staff Development" provide a sense of the changing definition of staff development. SPEC Flyer No. 18 summarizes the scene as of mid-1975:

> Staff development programs at one time were comprised mostly of informal job training, tuition assistance, and conference attendance policies. . . . Present staff development programs are more frequently intended to develop specific job capabilities for existing and projected library operations. . . . Reports coming from libraries which participated in the Management Review and Analysis Program (MRAP) indicate that staff development activities may be assuming a higher priority [than in the past] among academic and research libraries. In many of those libraries where a formalized staff development program did not exist, staff have recommended its establishment.[2]

By mid-1981, a period of universal retrenchment in libraries, the emphasis on training had further intensified, according to SPEC Flyer NO. 75:

> Efforts to strengthen staff development activities at ARL member libraries have continued over the past three years despite curtailed financial resources and, in some cases, reductions in staff. Changes in technology, staffing and work flow patterns, administrative structures, library systems and procedures, and academic programs have called for skills training in new areas and have posed the challenge of finding ways to provide this training with limited resources. . . . Some of the major changes in the past few years in staff development activities are: emphasis on skills training for supervisors and managers; an increase in the number of workshops and training programs devoted to human relation skills; incorporation of planning for individual staff development in the library's performance appraisal program; more training in technical skills associated with on-line computer systems; inter-institutional cooperation in planning and funding of staff training; involvement of more staff at all levels in planning and conducting training activities; use of job exchange programs to expand skills development opportunities to different categories and levels of staff. . . .[2]

...BUT DO THEY WORK?

So staff development programs, particularly training programs, are on the rise in response to the increased pace of change in our work environment, but so are the articles about "transfer failure," or how and why those training programs do not work. Transfer failure occurs when the learner in a training session is unable to transfer what was learned in the classroom to the workplace. It is based on the premise that it is possible for a person to be knowledgeable about a useful technique or about an effective attitude and how to apply it, and yet not practice what that person preaches. How many managers do you know, for example, who can articulate well the importance of "participatory decision-making," but who themselves manage top-down operations? Or who have read and believe the message of *The 1-Minute Manager*, but fail at giving constructive criticism and praise? Or, on a more universal level, who among us couldn't stand to reduce our intake of foods high in cholesterol or fat content despite our awareness that such foods shorten our lives?

I suspect that most libraries have no idea whether their training programs result in transfer failure or success. While no library today is rich enough to squander precious money and staff time on training that doesn't stick, we pay little attention, if any, to the long-term results of our training programs. Training is regarded as complete when the workshop was attended. Evaluation of staff development programs usually stops at analyzing the forms that the participants filled out at the program day's end, or very soon after. The program is regarded as "successful" or "worthwhile" if the majority of participants give it high marks. As sincere as the participants may be, those positive ratings say nothing about the long-term effectiveness of the program. The real test of a program's success is whether or not the trainee is using the new knowledge six months after attending the program.

Is the manager using the skills learned in a session on how to delegate responsibility? Does the front line staff member handle difficult patron encounters better because of techniques learned in a workshop dealing with angry patrons? Is the accountant using the special features learned in a class on spreadsheet software class? Is the reference librarian handling questions more efficiently by searching the databases covered in an online ready-reference seminar? When the answer is "no," not only has the desired change in the trainee not occurred, but also the expected impact on the organization will not occur. When our staff development programs fail to develop staff, we shouldn't be surprised if staff cynically regard such programs as nothing more than opportunities to get out of the office nor should we jump to conclusions about their intransigence if they resist attending them at all.[3] Under these circumstances, change in the workplace is slow and rough. Under different circumstances it can be timely and smooth.

MAKING THE TRAINING SESSION THE MIDDLE OF THE PROCESS

"Staff development" implies that a change will happen over time. That is, the word "development" suggests "progress," "evolution," "formation," "growth" — concepts of change that span a relatively long interval of time. Our library staff development programs, however, do not generally require more than a one-shot commitment of the learner's time: the 2-hour class, the one-day workshop, the 3-day retreat. Simply left at that, "transfer failure" can be expected; change — individual or organizational — is unlikely.

For transfer to be successful, there needs to be a "before" and an "after"; and activities need to involve more than the trainer and the trainee.[4] Throughout the training process — Before Training, During Training, and After Training — a five-way partnership should ideally develop between:

1. The trainer;
2. The trainee;
3. The person to whom the trainee reports, the "supervisor";
4. The library administration, and
5. The trainee's coach.

BEFORE TRAINING

Nine Prerequisites to the Training Session

Below are nine steps involving the five partners that will contribute to the success of the training, or retraining program.

1. The library administration articulates the expected outcome of a training program, relating the outcome to one or more library goals. This step presupposes that the library has some stated goals and a sense of what it takes to reach them. The term "staff development" invites the question, "development toward what?," but the reality is that the goal of most staff development programs, if defined at all, is too often narrowly limited to the perspective of the trainer, and should be broadened to fit in with the "big picture."

Example

Library goal: Patron satisfaction with library service whether or not the library is able to provide what was requested.
Workshop objectives: To support public service staff in achieving the library goal of patron satisfaction. To learn principles and techniques of providing consistent, high-quality, "professional" service regardless of the patron's need, personality or mood of the moment or those of the staff member.
Expected change: For participants—improved skills in dealing with patrons; For library—improved image by patrons as measured by decrease in complaints, increase in donor support, patron cooperation.

2. The library administration verifies the credentials of the trainer.

3. The trainer has a good understanding of the library's objectives in scheduling the program, based on discussions with a representative of the library administration, and tailors the program to suit the objectives.

4. The trainer includes in the publicity or call to the session information about the objectives of the program and how they relate to the library goal; a description of what will be covered; and the intended audience.

5. The trainee and the supervisor agree with the library goal(s) being addressed as well as the objectives of the workshop. If the trainee is being asked to abandon outdated practices, the supervisor expresses a sincere respect for those practices.

6. The trainee sees the need for the expected change and believes the session will be a beneficial step toward effectuating change.

7. The supervisor sees the need for the expected change that the session addresses, and believes the session will have a positive impact on the trainee's work and the functioning of the organization. Ideally, the supervisor has already attended the session; speaking from experience increases the supervisor's credibility.

8. The trainee and the supervisor discuss the types of change to expect as a result of the session.

9. The trainee and the supervisor plan how follow-up will take place after the session. As part of the follow-up plan, the trainee is paired with a coach, who will provide constructive feedback as the trainee practices after the session what was learned. The coach may be another participant in the training session, forming a kind of "buddy system" in which each agrees to coach the other, or, if the hierarchical relationship doesn't interfere, the supervisor; or a co-worker; or a total stranger.

DURING TRAINING

Four Ingredients to Promote Transfer

In addition to using skills that are expected of competent trainers (well-organized, well-paced, and enthusiastically-delivered presentations; attractive handouts; readable visuals—to mention a few), the trainer should include these elements in any training program:

1. The trainer reviews the evaluation form at the start of the session. Participant can then make mental notes throughout the session of components of their answers.

2. The trainer leaves time at the end of the program for participants to plan, in writing, how they will follow up after the session. This may be done on a separate form, or it may be done as part of the evaluation. The trainee should be able to keep a copy of the plan and should expect to share it with the supervisor. The trainer should

inform participants at the beginning of the program abut the follow-up plan.

3. When writing the follow-up plan, the trainee is encouraged to be as specific as possible about what was learned, and what will be practiced and applied.

4. The trainer providers time and experience that allow the participants to try out what was learned.

AFTER TRAINING

Follow-up Steps to Ensure Transfer

For training to "stick" the following steps are important to implement.

1. The supervisor provides a continued learning environment for the trainee. The supervisor discusses with the trainee the trainee's follow-up plan and together they decide how that can best be accommodated. The supervisor assures that there will be no blame for mistakes.

2. The trainee and the coach agree about what will be practiced. To the extent that the coach is uninformed about what the trainee has learned, the trainee is very specific about what the coach should look for. For example, the trainee in supervisory skills might appoint a supervisor as coach and say to the coach, "Listen for me to give specific praise after you've completed a job. I learned that was a weak point for me. . . . " Or, a manager who was trained in how to be more creative might say to a coach, "Be sure to tell me if I use a phrase such as 'we've tried that before' in responding to someone's idea. I'm not supposed to say that." Or, a staff member who took a class in making effective presentations and is rehearsing an upcoming presentation before a coach might say, "watch for me to make eye contact all around the room; and tell me every time I say 'uh'."

3. The trainee's coach balances criticism about what was done wrong with praise about what was done right.

4. The trainee gives the supervisor periodic progress reports.

5. The administration repeats the training programs frequently until a critical mass of employees competent in the desired skill is attained. The critical mass will have been reached when those who

possess the skill set the dominant standard, thereby achieving the desired change. Those in the minority who do not possess the skill can be expected to take responsibility to close the apparent gap between them and the dominant group.

STAFF DEVELOPMENT IN PERSPECTIVE

Library staff development programs have been well-intentioned but too shallowly conceived. On the one hand, we recognize that the skills required to provide library service are largely learnable. That is what keeps librarianship in the category of "professional schools," alongside nursing, law, medicine and architecture. On the other hand, we know that the occupation nowadays is in constant flux, requiring us to learn new skills and take on new work assignments within new organizational structures. Our staff development programs have expanded to begin to meet the challenge by a greater emphasis on training. However, we need to go further by expanding the scope of our staff development programs to expect change while maintaining continuity to the past. The beauty of taking staff development seriously is that the more we involve ourselves with the programs that help us move smoothly through particular changes, the more we learn about how to work constructively with change itself; the easier it is to keep ourselves learning and liking to learn; the greater the likelihood that we will replace our need for stability with a sense of control over change that includes the possibility of NOT making changes; and the readier we will be to respond to change by constructive participation in problem solving rather than by stagnation through resistance.

In sum, our response to change has up to now been stepped-up staff development programs with a focus on training; we need now to move to training programs that focus on change.

NOTES

1. Janet Paulk, "An interview with Sheila D. Creth," *Library Administration and Management* (June 1988): 117.
2. Association of Research Libraries. Office of Management Studies. SPEC Flyer Nos. 18, 1975 and 75, 1981.

3. For perspectives on resistance to change, see Rosabeth Moss Kanter's list of 10 reasons why employees resist change and tactics for dealing with them in "Managing the human side of change," *Management Review* (April 1985): 52-55; and Anne G. Lipow's discussion of resistance in "Why training doesn't stick: Who is to blame?" in *Proceedings of the 29th Allerton Institute* (November 1985) in press.

4. For a comprehensive discussion of transfer of training, see "How to overcome the transfer problem," in Julius E. Eitington *The Winning Trainer* (Houston, TX: Golf Pub. Co., 1984), 254-265. Also, check out the articles cited by Deborah Carver in "Transfer of training," *Library Administration and Management* (June 1988): 151-153.

The Technicolor Coat of the Academic Library Personnel Officer: The Evolution from Paper-Pusher to Policy Maker

Dana C. Rooks

INTRODUCTION

Personnel administration is a relatively new specialized function in libraries. Ten years ago, the position of Library Personnel Officer existed predominantly within only the largest academic libraries. Library school offerings on the subject of personnel administration range from cursory mention within a library administration course to a specialized seminar offered on a periodic basis. Even rarer is that library school student who will profess a desire and interest in seeking a position as library personnel officer.

Because the job of library personnel officer is so new, there are wide areas of disagreement as to its proper role and functions. While most libraries define the role of reference librarians or catalogers along similar lines, there is no common understanding of the appropriate responsibilities of the library personnel officer. Typically, the role of the personnel administrator is defined within each library initially in terms of the reasons the library administration established such a position and secondly, in terms of the individual selected for the position.

Initially, the position of library personnel officer was created primarily to serve a recordkeeping function. The increasing demands for documentation related to personnel actions brought about by

---

Dana C. Rooks is Assistant Director for Administration at the University of Houston Libraries.

© 1989 by The Haworth Press, Inc. All rights reserved.

legislation and the need to centralize routine activities regarding personnel practices in large libraries led to creation of the library personnel officer position in many libraries.

This paper addresses the dramatic changes which have occurred in the role of the personnel officer in academic libraries today. Just as libraries and librarians are involved in a rapid transformation from being keepers of knowledge to brokers of information, so too are personnel administrators evolving from the keepers of records to skilled managers of the library's human resources.

THE CHANGE TO HUMAN RESOURCE MANAGERS

Survival has become a primary objective within many academic libraries today. Costs of books and journals are increasing at several times the rate of inflation. The push to acquire technology to computerize both operations and services is growing ever stronger. The demands by library clientele for more information, delivered more efficiently, more conveniently, and at less cost, are intensifying. Simultaneously, the competition for highly skilled staff to manage and operate the increasingly complex business of libraries is escalating.

Given these new pressures, a library can no longer afford to ignore the need for human resource manager or to view the personnel function as little more than simple filing, housekeeping, and recordkeeping. The personnel function is complex and multifaceted. The human resource manager must be an integral part of the library's decision-making and policy-making structure.

It is people that do the work and create the ideas that allow the library to survive. It is people that limit or enhance the ability of the library to achieve its mission. The library personnel officer has a major role in achieving and sustaining the effectiveness of the library's most valuable asset—its human resources.

The transformation of the library personnel officer from paperpusher to human resource manager is characterized by the proliferation of roles that this individual must now assume. While not all library personnel managers will be required to fill each role, they will find themselves assuming many of these functions. The number of functions required will vary with the size of the library, the nature of its parent organization, the centralization or decentralization of specific functions, and the nature of the workforce. However, regardless of the specific roles that apply within an individual library, the common theme is the demanding and critical nature of each role to the success of the library as an organization. Each role is unique, each requires its own set of skills, and each is an important component of an effective overall human resource management program.

STAFF DEVELOPMENT OFFICER

The responsibility for staff training and development is one of the most common elements within the job description for library personnel officers and is frequently one of the justifications given for creating such a position within the library.

Typically the personnel officer will be expected to develop training programs to meet one or more of the following overall goals:

- To orient new employees to the organization and their jobs.
- To improve employees' performance levels on their present jobs.
- To enable employees to adapt to job changes.
- To prepare employees for new jobs.

While the role of staff development officer appears to be relatively straightforward and unambiguous, this belies the true complexity of this function. To be effective, the library's staff development officer must be involved in developing library-wide policies regarding employee development and in achieving an organizational commitment to those policies. The personnel officer must work with library supervisors and managers to analyze and identify employee training and development needs; recommend and obtain sufficient funds to support training and development efforts; assist in the formulation of individual employee development plans; identify suitable training opportunities within the university, the area, the state, or on a national level that would be of interest and benefit to employees; plan, design, and frequently, conduct in-house training programs; and evaluate the results of the overall employee development effort as well as specific training programs that are offered.

While accomplishing the objectives listed above, the personnel/ staff development officer must be cognizant of and responsive to the complex individual, professional, and environmental influences which affect the planning and evaluating of employee development activities. For example, training is critical in preparing women and minorities for advancement into new jobs, thus helping to fulfill equal employment opportunity and affirmative action requirements. Labor unions may also bargain for certain types of training to move members into better-paying jobs. The role of training and development in creating an environment of motivation among employees cannot be overstated. Yet another influence on employee development efforts is market conditions. Skills that are in short supply in the library marketplace may have to be developed in-house rather than recruited and hired on the open market.

The role of staff development officer may be a generally accepted responsibility for the library personnel officer, but the skills involved in successfully fulfilling this role are frequently underestimated. Successful staff training and development program require that the personnel officer also assume the roles of salesman, planner, forecaster, budget officer, negotiator, liaison, career counselor, mentor, evaluator, and trainer.

RECRUITER

Responsibility for recruiting new personnel is another common job component among library personnel officers. Recruitment is the process of identifying and attempting to attract individuals in the external labor market who are qualified for and interested in filling available job vacancies. Recruitment is an independent process from selection, but the role of the recruiter is essential. The selection of personnel can be no better than the pool of candidates generated by the recruitment effort.

Most library personnel officers regard recruitment as a significant activity. The failure to generate an adequate number of qualified job candidates can be costly to the library in many ways. It leads to lost production while the vacancy is re-advertised or, in some cases, to the lowering of hiring standards in an attempt to fill the void. In turn, lower-quality appointments mean additional costs for employee development and supervision to attain satisfactory levels of performance.

The job of recruiter calls into play a number of other roles. For example, equal employment opportunity laws and regulations are major influences in recruitment. Labor organizations and civil service agreements should be considered. Economic and labor market influences must be taken into account. Many of these roles will be discussed in subsequent sections of this paper.

In most libraries which have an office of library personnel, it is this individual or office which assumes the major responsibility for recruitment. The library personnel officer typically develops policy, strategies, and procedures in this area, processes and screens applications, and monitors the entire hiring process for effectiveness, efficiency, and compliance with appropriate laws and regulations.

The role of recruiter is critical to the continued success and development of the library. The ideal recruitment program is one that attracts a relatively large number of qualified applicants who will accept positions with the organization if offers are extended. The task sounds simple but it too belies the complexities. In order to succeed, the recruiter must fully understand what types of employees are needed, where and how to look for individuals with appropriate qualifications and interests, how best to "sell" the organization and the job, what inducements to use, or avoid, for various types of applicants, and how to distinguish applicants who are unqualified from those who have a reasonable chance of success.

If it is true that an organization is only as effective as its staff then the role of recruiter is indeed a crucial one.

COUNSELOR

The role of counselor is rarely included as a specific responsibility within the formal job description for the library personnel officer. Yet counseling is an activity which most library personnel officers engage in and, in some cases, one to which they devote considerable time and effort. Similarly, it is a role that many employees expect the personnel officer to assume. The question becomes what form this role should take and whether the library personnel officer is the appropriate individual, based on qualifications and training, to assume the role of counselor.

The term counseling covers a wide variety of situations ranging from professional counseling to routine information giving. Library personnel officers must be keenly aware of the extent and limitations of their skills and knowledge in each counseling situation and be prepared to refer the employee to an appropriate source when these limitations are exceeded.

Most counseling situations fall into one of three general areas. The first of these is vocational guidance. Vocational guidance may involve job or career counseling. In the area of job counseling, the library personnel officer would certainly be expected to be knowledgeable about opportunities and jobs within the library, including what the requirements are, how the promotion system operates, and what career ladders may exist for varying groups of employees. On the other hand, if an employee doubts that he or she is in the right career or wishes to switch careers completely, or if an employee is undecided about the overall direction that should be taken, professional vocational guidance is in order. Frequently vocational counselors within the university may be available to provide such services to university employees as well as students.

The temptation for the library personnel officer to provide vocational counseling to employees is a strong one, and is frequently reinforced by the apparent absence of available alternatives. The desire to serve as coach or mentor to staff is common among personnel officers. However, the appropriateness of that role will largely depend upon the individual's experience, skills, and training for the role.

The second general area of counseling involves providing information. These questions usually focus on the library or the university and include questions regarding policies, procedures, rules, services, benefits, etc. Questions may be job-related concerning work rules, job descriptions, salary issues or classification structures. They may require explanation or interpretation of library or university policies such as vacation or sick leave, outside employment, work hours, or leaves of absence.

Information regarding university benefits ranging from medical insurance to day-care facilities to retirement planning will be another source of questions confronting the library personnel officer in the role of counselor. Care should be taken here to ensure that these questions are addressed accurately and completely with referral to university benefits counselors when appropriate.

The final generalized area of counseling needs will fall into the area of personal problems which will often require professional counseling. No library personnel officer should be expected, or attempt, to counsel employees with personal problems, whether emotional or mental. The personnel officer is not a qualified counselor on marital problems, delinquent adolescents, emotional stress, or mental illness. The untrained personnel officer may, indeed, do the employee and the organization a great deal of harm if he or she assumes the role of the professional psychological counselor.

The role of the personnel officer as counselor is a role which all personnel officers will be expected to assume on a frequent basis by both staff and management. The key is to know the parameters or the boundaries within which the personnel officer can effectively serve as counselor. When the needs of the employee extend beyond these limits, the proper role of the personnel officer is as a resource for referral to an appropriate source for assistance.

ADVOCATE

One of the most difficult roles assumed by the academic library personnel officer is that of advocate. Is the personnel officer an ombudsman for the staff or a representative of the administration? The answer is *frequently both*.

The staff, justifiably, perceive the role of the personnel officer as counselor, liaison to the supervisors, managers, and administration of the library and even to the parent organization, champion of staff concerns and issues, and ombudsman for the resolution of conflicts. Simultaneously, the personnel officer is clearly a member of the administration charged with protecting and furthering the interests of the organization.

This is a conflict which is common to library personnel officers and one which is not easily resolved. This conflict of interest can be illustrated in the example of the employee involved in a disciplinary action. The personnel officer is typically in the position of advising both parties involved in the action. The supervisor has asked for advice on how to handle the problem employee, how to properly document the action, and what action can or should be taken. The employee also may have solicited the advice and counsel of the personnel officer on what rights he or she may have, what avenues are available for appealing the action, or possibly just in hopes of finding a sympathetic listener.

The difficult aspect of the role of advocate is that the personnel officer is asked to be both advocate for the employee and the management simultaneously. In some instances this can be accomplished. Employees have specific legal rights as specified within federal, state, and municipal laws and regulations, union contracts, civil service procedures, or institutional policies. In such instances the job of the personnel officer is to ensure compliance with these regulations, thus protecting the library from potential legal or governmental action.

More frequently the dual advocacy role of the personnel officer is less convergent. The skills of the personnel officer will ultimately determine how narrow or how wide the gap in the separation of the roles of employee advocate and management representative. Objectivity, flexibility, and creativity combined with effective skills in negotiation, persuasion and communication can make the personnel officer's role as advocate an essential tool of both staff and management.

FORECASTER

The ability to identify and plan for the staffing needs of the organization on both a short- and long-term basis is a primary element in measuring the success of the organization. Thus another important role of the library personnel officer is as a forecaster of manpower needs.

Human resource planning or manpower planning has been defined as the process of "getting the right number of qualified people into the right job at the right time."[1] Essentially all libraries engage in human resource planning, either formally or informally. However, most libraries which do manpower planning on an ad hoc basis omit two key components of the process of effective manpower forecasting.

1. Forecasts are limited to short-term needs, with no consideration of intermediate and long-term needs.
2. No comprehensive strategy is developed to ensure that these future needs can be met.

The role of the library personnel officer is to look beyond the next vacancy, to project personnel needs beyond the next budget cycle, and to integrate human resource planning into the library's basic long-range planning process.

All library managers should view human resource forecasting and planning as one of their most important and accountable job responsibilities. However, in the pressure of day-to-day operations, this is often not the case. The role of the personnel officer is to provide the structure, the impetus, and the assistance to the individual managers and supervisors to allow manpower forecasting to become an integral part of the planning process. This process will involve defining what skills and expertise will be needed to meet future objectives, analyzing current skills available among the staff in terms of the projected needs and thus determining the net requirements necessary to achieve long-range objectives. The process of long-range personnel forecasting will help eliminate surprises, minimize the number of crises that must be dealt with, and provide the library with a strong management tool for effecting change.

The second aspect of manpower forecasting is the more difficult job. This involves the development and implementation of a strategy to meet the needs identified in the planning process. Forecasting is more than a numbers game; it must also deal with issues in career planning, recruiting, and training and development. An effective program of manpower planning will ensure that the library is able to recruit, motivate, develop, retain, and utilize employees in an optimal manner to the benefit of both.

The failure to take action to meet future human resource needs will create barriers to future development of library programs and services resulting in costly delays in meeting new demand. Staff with the necessary skills to carry out future objectives will not have been developed internally nor will they have been recruited externally. Talented staff currently within the organization will have left the library because no opportunities existed to further their development.

The library personnel officer must assume a leadership role in human resource forecasting and planning. As libraries become increasingly more complex organizations, as the world of information technology becomes increasingly sophisticated, and as the demands on library collections and services escalate, the skills and abilities required of library staff will continue to change and the library administration will look increasingly to the library personnel officer to assume the primary role of forecaster and planner for short- and long-range human resource needs.

PARALEGAL

EEO, Title VII, FLSA, NLRB, ERIAS, and IRAC^2 may not be common library acronyms, yet each impacts significantly on the day-to-day operations of the library and governs many of the policy- and decision-making processes within the library.

The expansion of government legislation and regulation governing employment practices has approached exponential growth in the past two decades. Today's employees enter the workplace under the complex and far-reaching umbrella of government protection. The library personnel officer today is expected to possess a working knowledge of federal, state, and municipal laws and regulations in all areas of employment from discriminatory hiring practices to conditions of employment to employee rights, prior to, during, and after employment with the library.

The need for expert legal counsel specializing in the field of labor law cannot be understated. However, it is not reasonable to expect legal counsel to be available on a daily basis to provide advice and counsel on all matters regarding day-to-day operations.

The role of the library personnel administrator is to maintain a working knowledge of relevant legislation and regulations and, more importantly, an awareness or sensitivity to potential legal implications of the personnel actions and practices of the library's administrators and managers. In effect, the personnel administrator must learn to practice preventive labor law, while recognizing the need for legal assistance at the appropriate time.

Issues of equal pay for equal work, minority rights, affirmative action programs, employment discrimination, unionization or civil service, arbitration, employee benefits, wage and hour laws, and immigration are only a few of the many areas of legislation affecting the human resource professional.

The paralegal role of the library personnel officer is an increasingly complex one to fulfill. Yet libraries and their governing bodies are becoming increasingly aware of the important role of the personnel officer in administering legislation and compliance. As Arthur Curley concluded,

> A knowledge of the law is hardly the chief talent required by a personnel manager; but insufficient knowledge of the legal structure that constitutes a framework within which personnel policies and practices must be contained can ultimately cripple an otherwise progressive and effective program of personnel management and development.[3]

LABOR RELATIONS OFFICER

The movement toward unionization in academic libraries is a fairly recent occurrence. As Theodore Guyton noted in his 1975 book on library unionization, professionals in college and university libraries are still not as extensively unionized as those in public libraries.[4] Yet labor unions for support staff, professional staff, or both are well-established in many large university libraries, as well as community college and four-year state and municipal college libraries.

While unions in libraries may be a more recent development, the civil service system has had a long history in libraries. As with unions, a civil service structure establishes strict guidelines for how managers hire, promote, discipline, and fire employees, as well as mandating salary administration for employees within the system.

The role of personnel officer in the library governed by union contracts or civil service systems is again a complex one involving contract negotiation, interpretation, and administration, as well as negotiation and resolution of conflicts and grievances. An often overlooked impact on the personnel officer in a union or civil service library is the time that must be devoted to working with union or civil service-related matters and representatives. If adequate staffing provisions have not been made, other personnel activities may, of necessity, suffer from inadequate attention.

Labor relations is frequently an emotionally-charged issue with strongly-held convictions on both sides. The skills required of the successful personnel officer in dealing with union or civil service issues must also embody an awareness or sensitivity to the concerns and convictions of both views and an ability to convey the opposing perception to each party.

The role of labor relations officer is yet another example of the expansion of responsibilities incorporated within the position of library personnel officer. The success and skills of the individual in handling these responsibilities will, to a large extent, determine the library's ability to successfully meet its objectives. The goal of the library personnel officer is to minimize labor strife, by establishing an environment which fosters mutual trust and understanding through communication, flexibility, and respect.

As Frederick Duda concluded, "If management does not make the effort to build bridges with the union, it will never meet its primary obligation of providing service to its clientele with any degree of distinction."[5] The library personnel officer must be a visible and effective voice in laying the foundation for these bridges.

MANAGER

As the job of library personnel officer has evolved from paper-pusher to policy maker, another major change in roles has occurred. From the one-person operation charged with recordkeeping responsibilities, the Office of Library personnel has grown to encompass a complex array of responsibilities within the arena of human resource management. As the responsibilities have expanded, additional staff positions and specialists have been added to handle the various components of the personnel services operation. Thus library personnel officers have, by virtue of necessity, assumed the role of managers of large staffs and large budgets.

The role of manager adds yet another dimension to the skills and abilities required of a successful library personnel officer. The individual personnel officer can no longer deal personally and directly with all aspects of human resource management. The personnel officer must understand the multifaceted objectives and activities of the personnel operation, but he or she must function as a manager of many of these operations and not in a staff role. Human resource managers must assess where their specialized skills and abilities can best be utilized and not devote their time to tasks which can be accomplished just as efficiently and in a more cost-effective manner by personnel office staff or specialists.

Relinquishing to other staff is often very difficult for library personnel officers. Since the evolutionary process occurred over a period of time, the personnel officer has been in a position of periodically assuming yet another new role as merely an addition to existing duties. When the load becomes too burdensome and the need for additional staff positions becomes apparent, the personnel officer is faced with the question of what to relinquish—recruitment, staff development, what? Many of these functions are roles which are enjoyable and challenging to personnel officers. The necessity to relinquish direct responsibility and assume a role as manager of one or more of these functions is often difficult.

Yet the evolution to more and increasingly complex responsibilities for library personnel officers has not concluded. The need for experienced human resource managers and specialists in academic libraries is only now beginning to be appreciated and understood.

CHANGE AGENT FOR THE FUTURE

Libraries and library staff members are experiencing a period of rapid and dramatic change brought about by the emergence of technology as a dominant force in all aspects of society. As libraries attempt to cope with the seemingly insatiable demands of their clientele for information, with decreasing budgets and increasing costs, and with growing competition from other sectors for the role of information provider, our survival will depend upon how well we adapt.

A key role for the personnel officer in the future will be as a change agent. The changes that are occurring in libraries will require new perspectives on the basic mission of libraries with redefined goals and objectives. In order to successfully achieve these new goals, libraries will be forced to reexamine their basic organizational structures and staffing patterns. New skills will be needed requiring retraining of current staff, on learning to deal with new staff with skills unfamiliar to the traditional world of libraries. As Jennifer Cargill and Gisela Webb point out, "libraries in transition will find the personnel officer a particularly important team player in effecting change within the organization."[6]

Qualified library personnel officers will be needed to deal with the stresses created by change and with the changing demands of the library staff for increased involvement and participation in the process of change. Personnel officers will be needed to take a leadership role in the planning and implementation of activities which will allow libraries to adapt and survive:

— staff development
— continuing education
— manpower planning
— recruitment
— management development
— organizational development
— labor relations
— communication
— policy making

The personnel officer plays a critical role in the library of the future. The perception of paper-pusher is no longer valid and evolution to policy maker is a reality.

REFERENCES

1. Charles F. Russ, Jr., "Manpower Planning Systems: Part I," *Personnel Journal* 61 (January 1982): 41.
2. Equal Employment Opportunity; Title VII of the Civil Rights Act of 1964;

National Labor Relations Board; Fair Labor Standards Act; Employee Retirement Income Security Act; Immigration Reform and Control Act.

3. Arthur Curley, "The Legal Framework of Personnel Administration," in *Personnel Administration in Libraries*, eds. Sheila Creth and Frederick Duda (New York: Neal-Schuman, 1981), p. 27.

4. Theodore L. Guyton, "Unionization: The Viewpoint of Librarians" (Chicago: American Library Association, 1975), p. 2.

5. Frederick Duda, "Labor Relations," in *Personnel Administration in Libraries*, eds. Sheila Creth and Frederick Duda (New York: Neal-Schuman, 1981), p. 180.

6. Jennifer Cargill and Gisela M. Webb, *Managing Libraries in Transition* (Phoenix, AZ: Oryx Press, 1988), p. 153.

Accountability of Human Resource Professionals

Frances O. Painter

We often speak of "being accountable." Human resources professionals, as well as other members of the library administrative team, are held responsible for carrying out certain obligations. When we are accountable for our work, we are held responsible for results; we can give satisfactory reasons for our decisions; we expect to be called to account to justify the trust and confidence, the good faith and candor involved in modern human resources management.

Today's human resources professionals expect to take an active role in the direction and management of the library. As members of the administrative team, we plan recruitment and staffing efforts. We design and direct staff development programs. We work with line managers to administer compensation programs that make it clear what type of performance is valued and rewarded in our library. We often provide our assessment of the human resources implications of proposed programs, such as a grant project for data conversion, or the introduction of new online information sources in the Reference Department. On a daily basis, we encounter problems of interpersonal conflict, interdivisional warfare, personal and departmental crises, difficulties working with a supervisor, or professional burnout. My cocktail party answer to the question, "What do you do?" has always been, "I make people see reality." In a more reflective mood, I would say that the job of any human resources professional is to assist others in understanding and starting to claim as their own the mission, values, and goals that are cur-

---

Frances O. Painter is Personnel Officer for the Libraries at the University of Virginia Tech, Blacksburg, VA.

rently driving the organization's objectives. The word "currently" is important—an ever-increasing part of the job is to encourage and support other people to function in an environment of continuing change.

There is much to contribute here towards a library's effectiveness. However, Personnel is a staff function, and measuring our contribution is different from performance evaluation or supervisory review elsewhere in our organization. Precise and timely measurement of results is harder to come by. Operational personnel management is a shared responsibility between the personnel office and the library supervisors and department heads. Personnel is a speciality function, not clearly understood in detail by our superiors, not always well-liked by our colleagues. Why should a human resources professional be concerned with accountability, being measured, being evaluated, allowing others to review our impact on organizational objectives?

Spencer has articulated well the negative feelings human resources professionals harbor toward evaluation:

- People do not know how. Quite a statement for a profession concerned with education, training, and development.
- Fear that evaluation will show that programs do not work, or are not worth their cost. This fear may be realistic. However, consider the benefits of examining your operations to see if your past efforts were successful, and to take action to improve or redesign activities. Your time is too valuable, and your credibility too important to waste in noncontributing programs.
- Beliefs that evaluative data or numbers are phony. This again can be a realistic fear. Healthy skepticism is always advisable when reacting to evaluative data. If your role in the organization has been an active one, you will be able to distinguish the smoke from the fires.
- Evaluation is not worth it. It takes too much time. Consider the traditional premise of cost-benefit analysis: You invest in getting better data for your decisions when that investment has a return in making better decisions about larger issues. Knowing how well employment activities are being performed will en-

able you to focus your efforts to recruit and attract the best people to your library.
- There is no real incentive to do it. A personnel program should be just as important to the library as other functions that we traditionally keep track of. We measure what is important to us. Our impact on the organization should call for awareness and visibility.[1]

Some of the benefits to be gained from an evaluation of the personnel function are obvious from the previous discussion. There is an old marketing adage: "Having lost sight of our objectives, we redoubled our efforts." The human resources professional needs information to improve performance and to know if the right things are being done, in the right way, at the right time. To be a significant resource to the library staff and management, we need to be effective. To maintain our own credibility, to be confident in our value to the organization, we need feedback. The most common frustration of human resources professionals is not knowing that we make a difference, not getting any information that our plans and programs really benefit anyone. Evaluation makes it clear to everyone, even ourselves, that the library values the problems, solutions, and results that pass through our offices day to day.

EVALUATION OF A PERSONNEL/HUMAN RESOURCES PROGRAM

The literature of personnel/human resources management reflects a concern for evaluation of the function side by side with the wealth of articles calling for leadership and significant participation in strategic management. The traditional personnel administration efforts such as employment, discipline, and managing standard payroll and benefit plans are often assessed in terms of how closely specific rules and procedures are followed. Recent years have seen the growth of human resources departments more closely associated with the organization's strategic planning and overall objectives, with a concern that HR management contribute in some measurable way to the overall success of the organization.

Gray has identified the four basic questions to consider when evaluating a personnel department in a frequently cited 1965 article. We have already explored his first point, why an evaluation is necessary. Gray's other three questions are: Who should do the evaluating? What criteria should *not* be used in making the evaluation? And finally, on what basis and by what methods should the department be evaluated?[2]

Human resources management has a role in every organizational unit in the library. Gray remarks that

> ... every employee, regardless of his point of vantage in the organization, immediately qualifies as his own expert on the merits and deficiencies of the Personnel Department. It can be safely said that no other area of the company's operations comes under more constant and more critical scrutiny by more people, both inside and outside the organization.[3]

Human resources professionals and the programs they administer are constantly being reviewed and evaluated by library directors, department heads, supervisors, and the newest online editor in Cataloging. All these individuals are affected directly and indirectly by human resources management, and to be accountable for our actions, we must give them the right to evaluate us. Most human resources professional report to a high level of management. This senior manager will take into account impressions from other sources in formally assessing the performance of the HR professional.

Gray's category of criteria that should *not* be used in evaluating personnel departments includes quantitative measures that are not good indicators of human resources success or failure, although they certainly may be symptoms that other problems exist. Gray lists turnover rates, personnel department expenses, whether or not there is union activity, and number of grievances as examples of these measures.[4] There is nothing wrong with tracking these items, but they must be used in reviews relative to other larger issues.

Where then to begin with an evaluation? Gray suggests looking at the principal activities assigned to the Personnel Department, such as recruitment, employment, training and development, appraisal, employee relations, and salary administration, and putting these functions in their proper place in support of the philosophy, principles, and policies of the organization. He suggests five methods to choose from, or to use in combination:

Observation by higher management. Even if you have no mechanism in place for evaluation of your practices, you will be evaluated by senior managers through observation. These constant mental notes may or may not be accurate, depending on how well you as a human resources professional have educated your colleagues and how well you have made your personnel objectives a part of the library's strategic plan. Also, like all good staff work, much HR administration is not noticeable when it's working. If you successfully avoid or reduce turnover, people problems, or EEO/AA concerns, senior management may be blissfully unaware of the work of an effective personnel department.

Formal appraisal by higher management. Your performance reviews with your boss are a chance for you to educate him or her of your value to the organization. You can market your services and highlight your accomplishments. You can confirm your priorities. Of course, you may also be told that the Cataloging Department is not getting the assistance from you they want, or your staff development program is not a priority item in this year's reduced budget.

Group discussion among "customers" of the Personnel Department. Gray suggests the group include one member of senior management; at least one or two first-line supervisors; two employees—one long-term and one newcomer; and a representative of the Personnel Department itself. After discussion, the group prepares a final report to be shared first with the personnel manager and later with senior management.

Opinion polls. Gray notes some words of caution here. Do not ask employee's opinions about conditions that cannot be changed. If your library staff are subject to a statewide graded salary system, there is little point in finding out what people think of it. Possible answers should be constructed carefully, with choices possible in a range from very favorable to the very unfavorable. Space should be provided for comment, since the commentary is often the most revealing part of such a poll.

Use of a consultant. All the usual advantages of employing a consultant apply here—a fresh, unbiased approach, confidentiality, and experience in other organizations.

Gray concludes that an evaluation of the personnel Department is inevitable; the only choice is whether the evaluation is formal and systematic, or by change and snap judgement.[5]

Appraisal of the Personnel Department by line management is a useful guide, because this group is in a unique position to assess not only the results of policies and procedures but also the effectiveness of the human resources professional. The ties are strong between HR professionals and the supervisors and department heads we serve, ties based on a two-way interchange of advice, information, and expertise. Leonard and Heneman have described an evaluation scale that could be adapted to a library setting, with attention to the authors' comments on item construction and uses of the scale.[6]

We know that managers and employees, and different levels of managers and supervisors will have different expectations of the human resources function. Tsui has explored this multiple constituency approach to evaluating the effectiveness of the human resources department.[7] She found large differences among the constituencies' expectations for appropriate activities for the personnel department, and among the constituencies' satisfaction with the personnel department's performance. The complex role played by human resources is highlighted in her statement that, "There is strong evidence to suggest the presence of incompatibility and conflict in the expectations held by the multiple constituencies."[8] Human resource professionals are accountable to both management and staff. We will examine the dual loyalties of human resources administration later in this article.

The American Society for Personnel Administration has published an *Audit Handbook of Human Resources Practices: Auditing the Effectiveness of the Human Resources Functions*.[9] The handbook is organized into the nine areas of human resources administration recognized by ASPA. Sections include descriptions of human resources objectives and goals, "red flags" or troublespots to be alert for, and questionnaires to audit and score your organization's programs. Action plans are provided with specific recommendations for improvement. The handbook's review and questionnaires could easily be used in group setting with various "customers" of the personnel department, as suggested by Gray.

An evaluation of the human resources function should be carried out periodically to ensure that programs and services offered are in tune with the changing environment within and without the library, not a review undertaken only when there is a crisis. The examination and study should seek to determine problem areas and recommend alternative action plans to improve human resources' overall effectiveness to the organization, as well as noting what activities are going well and should be continued. Employee morale surveys have their place in assessing the need for uncovering employee relations programs, but reactions of how staff "feel" about a HR policy or activity are often influenced by the way line managers and supervisors conduct their day-to-day personnel business. They should not be used as the only means of review for the HR function.

EVALUATION OF THE PERSONNEL/HUMAN RESOURCES PROFESSIONAL

The personal style of the personnel/human resources professional often sets the tone for the entire function. The professional's skill and influence with other administrators often determine the power available to develop human resources skills throughout the organization, and to initiate change. Albert Vicere has identified seven critical professional must develop, and these same areas should be covered in a performance review:

Knowledge of the organization's major business functions. A library human resources professional should know what goes on in technical services, reference services, and automation or systems operations, particularly to know their programs in terms of implications and consequences for employment, motivation, and performance evaluation.

Awareness and anticipation of organizational needs in a changing environment. An understanding of automation and technology currently in use and future requirements is one area for the HR professional to be aware of and prepare for changing requirements for staffing and training.

Knowledge of the human relations function itself, especially the ability to design and implement solutions to problems. Education and experience in personnel administration ought to enable the professional to maintain a state of relative peace, quiet, and consistency. However, the rapidly shifting priorities of our modern workplaces demand more than just getting things right if human resources professionals are to really help our supervisors manage a diverse group of 1980s workers. We need to be able to provide creative solutions to the personnel management problems brought to use — how to motivate, to lead, to involve our older staff, to recognize quality performance, to make do with less.

Ability to develop effective human resources plans and programs in support of organizational strategy. To have significant impact on the mission of the library, we need to understand our library's organizational culture and to develop human resources plans clearly linked to goals and objectives.

Ability to implement these plans and programs. A human resources professional must work effectively with supervisors and managers throughout the library to effectively promote and "sell" sound personnel management practices. Most of our positions are staff positions, with no direct authority. Our power is largely based on relationships — we provide useful information, good analysis and helpful solutions to others. These people in turn learn to trust and respect us, and to be willing to listen and be influenced by us. A HR professional needs a network of friends, supporters, colleagues, and professional contacts.

Ability to communicate, make sound decisions, and provide leadership within the organization. Management and leadership skills such as high energy level, listening skills, the ability to maintain a confidence, to negotiate, to coach and support others, and the ability to communicate ideas clearly and logically both orally and in writing are no less important to a HR manager than to our line counterparts.[10]

The evaluation of the human resources professional should have the same characteristics of any well-designed performance appraisal system. The appraisal should identify weak and strong areas, with an emphasis on seeking specific ways to improve performance. A formal appraisal should represent only one focused communication between evaluator and employee, since communication concerning performance should be a continuous process of clarifying and specifying to an individual what is expected of him/her on the job. The HR professional can benefit from conscientious evaluation with the goal of improving performance and developing skills. While results of an evaluation of the HR program may be shared judiciously with others in the organization to highlight administrative support for a quality program, the personal evaluation of the HR professional is best kept private and confidential between the professional and his/her immediate supervisor.

THE PERSONNEL EFFECTIVENESS GRID

In the 1960s Blake and Mouton introduced the concept of the Managerial Grid as a means of increasing leadership effectiveness. The concept has been developed further in a succession of books and articles, including the Grid for social workers, for nurses, and for academic administrators.[11] Blake and Mouton's original grid dimensions were:

1. Concern for Production, and
2. Concern for People.

Peterson and Malone have addressed the multiple constituencies and dual role of human resources administration in their Personnel Grid, as:

1. The support given personnel/human resources by top management, and
2. The support and cooperation for personnel/human resources policies and programs by operating all through the organization.

Combining these two with a third variable, the HR staff's perceived qualifications, Peterson and Malone suggest their Personnel Effectiveness Grid can be used as a model for measuring personnel/HR departments performance.[12]

Imagine a graph with "Support and Influence of Personnel with Top Management" on the y-axis; "Cooperation and Support for Personnel Staff" on the x-axis; and a third dimension, "Personnel

Qualifications and Quality of Programs." On the one hand the library HR professional must support the library policy, the rules and procedures, the administration, department heads, and supervisors. On the other hand, personnel management must be concerned with the library staff at all levels throughout the organization. I will use the Peterson and Malone model and try to clarify the working style of library HR professionals and how this "dual citizenship" affects our accountability.

The upper left-hand corner of the Personnel Effectiveness Grid would represent a high level of support for HR on the part of management, but a low level of support and cooperation at subordinate levels of the organization. Human resources would enjoy the borrowed power and influence of the library administration, but some staff may combine their deference with resentment. Genuine cooperation may not be widespread enough to permit human resources professional to become involved in giving advice and problem solving. This scenario is often characterized by:

- The HR professional's desire for acceptance, approval, or validation from his/her colleagues in management. Power and control become important.
- Greater emphasis on personnel's auditing and control functions. The HR department is often called upon to track measurements and standards and ensure compliance with policy. The department runs a "tight ship" with the emphasis on stability. Checking on employee performance is indispensable, and discipline is more punishment than performance improvement.
- Management may turn over too much of the daily business of good employee relations to the HR function. The HR professional may encourage this overdependence rather than develop responsible, skilled line managers.
- Staff may see the HR professional as a "spy" for management. Ideas and suggestions will be met with skepticism and suspicion. Supervisors will love to say "I tried what you told me to do and it didn't work!" The Personnel Department receives no real understanding, commitment, or enthusiasm for its programs.

- There will be lip service for personnel programs, but ideas not put into daily practice. A few "showcase" programs that the director can talk about and be recognized for will be encouraged.

The lower left quadrant represents the old view of human resources management—routine clerical support and services are delivered, but the Personnel Department has limited influence or support with either management or staff. Line managers live to tell horror stories about working with the "idiots" and "petty bureaucrats" in Personnel.

- Human resources staff are often accused of tunnel vision, of being the only ones who value their duties and methods. Records and paperwork in the Personnel Department become as sacred as the cataloger's old card file shelflist.
- Personnel programs are relatively modest both in cost and benefits. Management considers the HR function adequate; other departments consider HR a necessary evil.
- HR staff go through the motions but have little real impact on organizational goals. Appearing to be truly uninvolved is more important than a concern for encouraging positive change.
- HR staff provide services and respond only to managers who bring needs to them. No one expects much, and not much is given.

The lower right quadrant is characterized by a low level of interest and support on the part of senior management, which has obliged the human resources department to "sell" itself to the lower levels of the organization. HR staff are extremely sensitive to the perceived needs of staff, perhaps emphasizing "feeling good" rather than positive change. This is a secure role for the HR professional, since relationships are friendly, and there is much approval and attention coming from the staff. I do not mean to suggest that being responsive to the needs of people in the organization is a negative thing. What goes wrong here is an overemphasis by the HR professional on deference, on being acquiescent to avoid the risk of conflict and rejection. Many creative ideas or forward-looking decisions may be postponed or overlooked for the sake of smoothing things over and preserving harmony.

- Human resources' counseling role is greatly expanded and is carried out well. Individuals are encouraged to talk about their feelings to a warm, nonjudgemental personnel staff. However, much-needed advice or suggestions for change may not be given because so much emphasis is placed on the personal and emotional. We have all joked about dealing with administrators, usually beloved old deans, who really didn't attend to our problems but made us feel good.
- Psychotherapy and counseling should be the realm of trained doctors, counselors, and social workers. While meaning well, most HR professionals cannot provide serious counseling for troubled individuals.
- Other departments' working relationships with the Personnel Department will tip the balance of power in favor of departmental decisions. Relationships are dependent on mutual admiration, and so may vary widely among departments. Everyday conduct of evaluation, use of sick leave, and access to development activities may differ considerably in each department. It can be a slippery slope from being permissive, to being a soft touch, to being "conned." Some staff will realize quickly that HR staff can be manipulated.
- The human resource department that emphasizes abstract qualities such as "feeling better," "coming together," or "enjoying work" is setting itself up with complicated outcomes to measure. Such a department will have difficulty demonstrating what it has actually done for the past year. Respect and support for HR programs may well deteriorate.

Now let's turn to the upper right corner—to what Blake and Mouton call the 9,9 manager, the "full partner" human resources professional—where senior management support is high and a high degree of cooperation and support for HR activities exist at the lower levels of the organization. Sound personnel management practices contribute to the total organization's success. Participation, involvement, and commitment are evident. This enjoyment and gratification does not come without effort. Human resources professionals operating here must develop the competencies required to make positive contributions to their organization and to take an active role in achieving goals and objectives and inspiring others to do so. As a result:

- The Personnel Department participates in planning and policy making at the highest level of the organization. The department has its own goals and objectives in sync with those of the larger organization.
- Human resources priorities reflect the needs of working groups throughout the organization, at all levels.
- HR staff respond effectively to special problems and changes within the organization. Versatile solutions are proposed to solve people problems within a consistent framework of human resources principles and practices.
- The human resource professional's role becomes one of working together with groups or individuals to solve problems or presenting good information, clarifying differences, confronting disagreement; or arriving together at mutual goals.
- Review and criticism are used to learn from experience, to suppress problems or blame.

Peterson and Moore also realized that the level of competence of the Personnel Department staff will have an effect on its acceptance and effectiveness. Professionally qualified and experienced staff are more likely to enjoy and cooperate at all levels.

WHAT, THEN, SHALL WE DO?

The human resources professional can, and must, take an active role in shaping expectations for his/her role in the organization. This activity need not be covert, devious, nor suspect in any way. We cannot be all things to all people. We cannot always meet everyone's expectations. Expectations change over time, and some changes are very subtle, never expressed openly. But if we are going to be accountable, we must be concerned with how well we are meeting organizational expectations. The way to do this is to assist in developing and forming others' ideas about our role in the organization and our performance.

I suggest that our accountability is enhanced when other employees see us at work, see us acting on our values, see what we think is important, see us plan, organize, and set priorities. Our superiors, colleagues, and working acquaintances can then have a better chance at distinguishing the important from the unimportant. Reduced to the basic, if we bring others' expectations of us more in line with what we know we should do as professionals, then we have a better chance of meeting those expectations, thus gaining more confidence, respect, and trust. We also will be better poised to ask for and receive the increased resources we need to develop and maintain effective human resources programs. What are some actions we can take?

- Human resources professionals should serve on committees and task forces at all levels of the organization. We should seek out opportunities to actively participate and to show that we are interested in advancing organizational goals and objectives. Our lofty ideal of personnel management often have clear meaning to others only when they are applied to specific daily situations.
- We should know the professional language, know what our organization does. A library HR professional should be able to discuss retrospective conversion, software migration, collection development workloads and their personnel implications. We must know what is going on in the daily work lives of those we want to help.
- We must be able to provide more than gut reactions to assist our colleagues in problem solving. Our professional knowledge must be up-to-date and responsive. We need to read professional literature, attend professional seminars, be in touch with a network of other HR professionals.
- We need to learn to be troubleshooters and to teach others the same skills. Libraries will always find people in confrontational situations who need to be guided to be aware of the needs of others, to listen, and to resolve differences. Avoiding

such differences limits the full participation of the library staff.
- Our own personnel staff, be it a one half-time secretary or two or more personnel assistants, must be qualified, participate in training in activities, and encouraged to be active and responsive.

By actively participating in both long-range planning and the daily operations of our libraries, we will hear what is going on—opinions, attitudes, and different ideas what we can deal with before we are called in as a last resort. Personnel as damage control is an attitude that hinders our focus on the real issues.

As human resources professionals, we will realize that every individual in the organizations will have open and not-so-open expectations of our role, and will give us varying degrees of support. When we are held accountable, when we are formally and casually evaluated, our report will not only tell us to "do more and do it better." Our less successful programs or our personal omissions or weaknesses will be approached with the intention of resolving them in a positive way. We will be more accountable when we have communicated both our competence and our credibility to managers and staff throughout the library.

NOTES

1. Lyle M. Spencer, Jr. *Calculating Human Resources Costs and Benefits: Cutting Costs and Improving Productivity* (New York: John Wiley & Sons, 1986): 4-5.
2. Robert D. Gray, "Evaluating the Personnel Department," *Personnel* (March-April 1965): 43.
3. Ibid., 43.
4. Ibid., 45-47.
5. Ibid., 49-52.
6. David A. Leonard and Herbert Heneman, Jr., "A Scale for Supervisory Evaluation of Personnel Departments," *Personnel* (November 1951): 229-235.
7. Ann S. Tsui, "Defining the Activities and Effectiveness of the Human Resources Department: A Multiple Constituency Approach," *Human Resources Management*, 26 (Spring 1987): 35-69. Anne S. Tsui and George Milkovich, "Personnel Department Activities: Constituency Perspectives and Preferences," *Personnel Psychology*, 40 (1987):519-537.
8. Tsui, "Defining the Activities and Effectiveness . . . ," p.63.

9. George E. Biles and Randall S. Schuler, *Audit Handbook of Human Resources Practices: Auditing Effectiveness of the Human Resources Functions*. (Alexandria, Virginia: American Society for Personnel Administration, 1986).

10. Albert A. Vicere, "Break the Mold: Strategies for Leadership," *Personnel Journal* (May 1987): 69-70.

11. Robert R. Blake and Jane S. Mouton, *The Managerial Grid III* (Houston, Gulf Publishing Company, 1985).

12. Donald J. Peterson and Robert L. Malone, "The Personnel Effectiveness Grid (PEG): A New Tool for Estimating Personnel Department Effectiveness," *Human Resources Management* (Winter 1975): 15.

For Product Safety Concerns and Information please contact our EU representative GPSR@taylorandfrancis.com
Taylor & Francis Verlag GmbH, Kaufingerstraße 24, 80331 München, Germany

www.ingramcontent.com/pod-product-compliance
Lightning Source LLC
Chambersburg PA
CBHW052131300426
44116CB00010B/1859